In Love with Life

Edmond Israel

IN LOVE WITH LIFE

AN AMERICAN DREAM
OF A LUXEMBOURGER

Interviewed by Raymond Flammant

Pampered child
Refugee
Factory worker
International banker

New Thinking

SACRED HEART UNIVERSITY PRESS
FAIRFIELD, CONNECTICUT
2006

IN LOVE WITH LIFE
An American Dream of a Luxembourger
by Edmond Israel

ISBN 1-888112-13-1

Copyright 2006 by the Sacred Heart University Press

This book is based on *La vie, passionnément*
Entretiens avec Raymond Flammant
French edition published in 2004 by
Editions Saint Paul, Luxembourg

*I dedicate these pages to all those
who brought light and warmth to my life.*

I thank my dear wife Renée for her counsel and advice.

*I express my particular appreciation to Raymond Flammant,
who asked me the right questions.*

*Thanks also to my assistant, Suzanne Cholewka Pinai,
for her efficient help.*

Contents

Foreword

The first time I met Edmond Israel was in June 1996, two days before he was to receive the degree, Doctor of Law, *honoris causa,* from Sacred Heart University at our campus in Luxembourg. He had been highly recommended for the degree by members of the Board of Regents, especially Henri Alhborn, a leading representative of the Luxembourg business and political community.

The purpose of our meeting was to be introduced to each other and to spend a few minutes chatting informally. It turned out to be so much more than that. More than two hours later we had engaged in an extraordinary discussion about the dialogue between science and religion, the implications of chaos theory for modern philosophy, the relationship between ethics and the global challenges of our times, as well as the current state of inter-religious dialogue between Christians and Jews. We both knew that we had just scratched the surface of our mutual intellectual interests and concerns. More important, we initiated a rich friendship that has grown ever-deeper over the ensuing years, to the point where we are now the best of friends. Our Friday afternoon exchange is now a tradition: I say to him, "Shalom

Shabbat," and he responds, "Shalom Sunday." We cherish our differences that make us stronger together.

Edmond Israel embraces the world as it is, while at the same time he delights in working for what the world can become. The unprecedented problems that challenge most of our major institutions and our traditional ways of doing things are so new that few of us have the courage or even the capacity to consider them. Yet Edmond Israel enthusiastically relishes the opportunity to think differently and boldly about how to hold our problems together in creative tension and wrestle with them until moral and efficient solutions can be found. For him, thinking in new ways is necessary for humanity to reach its highest potential and this requires a constant reappraisal and revision of the conventional ways we live and work in the world.

Edmond Israel's life represents an extraordinary example of the best of Western humanism. He is an outstanding business leader, but even more important, he is a remarkable human being whose heart is compassionate and full of joy. Edmond knows the depth of the journey into self-discovery and how those who walk that road are tested by the fire of adversity. He has seen the worst and best of times and chooses to believe in the highest capacity of humans. A master teacher, he challenges people to deeper reflection on what they are doing and why they are doing it. He playfully and purposefully invites others into the deeper meanings and joys of life. He does not insist that you agree with his beliefs or opinions, he merely asks that you listen to his stories and respond with your own.

Recently, Edmond visited Sacred Heart University's campus in Fairfield, Connecticut, and his energy and upbeat personality were apparent to all. He seemed to embody the humble but increasingly generative human power so well-described by Robert F. Kennedy:

Few will have the greatness to bend history; but each of us can work to change a small portion of events, and in the total of all those acts will be written the history of this generation. . . . It is from numberless diverse acts of courage and belief that human history is thus shaped. Each time a man stands up for an ideal, or acts to improve the lot of others, or strikes out against injustice, he sends forth a tiny ripple of hope, and crossing each other from a million different centers of energy and daring, those ripples build a current which can sweep down the mightiest walls of oppression and resistance.

While visiting Sacred Heart, Edmond reminded us that the meaningful life is one of thoughtfulness, generosity, and love, and he continues to do what he has always done: take enjoyment in each new day with all of its challenges and possibilities. All these qualities are on full display in his fascinating memoir, *La vie, passionnément*, published in 2004 in French. The Sacred Heart University Press is very proud to publish an English edition of this book, prepared by the author, because we see in Edmond Israel a living example of wisdom and hope in a world where both are desperately needed. *In Love with Life* is a wonderful and inspiring read, and urges us all to think in new ways, to love with depth, and to take action guided by those simple but ever-challenging and ever-rewarding principles.

Anthony J. Cernera, Ph.D.
President, Sacred Heart University

Preface

For many years a number of my friends kept on insisting and even harping: "You must write your memoirs. You lived in an interesting time, a great part of the twentieth century and (this is my personal addition) hopefully a quite extensive part of the twenty-first century." I must confess that I hesitated consistently, primarily for two reasons:

First, there is a sort of nostalgia, of profound sadness, which penetrates me when I have to plunge into the past.

Then, probably the most important reason is that I am really lazy. It takes me a long time before I set myself to a task. But when I do it I become intensely immersed in my work. My natural impatience gets hold of me and I want the job to be done quickly in order to return to my natural state of laziness, a state when my grey cells keep on vibrating while I am enjoying the more futile moments of life.

It is my friend and interviewer, Raymond Flammant, who was able to dispel my hesitations and doubts.

The love of life is the engine which makes me function. It has been a red thread during the sometimes turbulent and perilous phases of my existence, which has also known moments of intense happiness. It is the love of life which has allowed me to confront the challenges and the dangers, practically from childhood until today and hopefully tomorrow.

As a matter of fact, I have lived several lives.

First, a pampered child within the fold of a very compact family radiating warmth and affection. Then refugee, blue-collar worker, banker, and finally constructing a philosophy, which I call "New Thinking." It was my father, who since my early childhood, ignited in me the urge and passion to explore the depths of all things, the passion to engage in the never ending quest of a true meaning. Thus I am some sort of an autodidact philosopher. At the same time my professional activities changed from factory worker in the United States by necessity into becoming a banker after the war in Luxembourg, all this by sheer coincidence and also by necessity.

Can I be a guide, some kind of a mentor for others? Personally I am reluctant in this respect. I am not very fond of pontificating, preaching morals and ethical behavior based on my own thinking and experiences. People tell me that the experiences of my life must necessarily lead to some kind of wisdom that I should share with others. I am not very convinced of this precisely because the environment undergoes constant changes, at an even faster pace in our time than previously. Heraclitus said "Nothing is permanent but change."

I rather see the purpose of this book to engage in a dialogue in the mind, and perhaps also in reality, between the author and the reader.

In the first and second part of this book entitled "Dancing on a Volcano" and "Surviving, Living, Constructing," I evoke my existence, sometimes dramatic, often dull. The third and last part, "New Thinking" consists of my reflections and thoughts for the construction of a positive and even promising future along the lines that I have already communicated in a number of conferences and lectures particularly to younger people.

The principle of my personal philosophy is based on what I believe is a law of nature. The arrow of time is pointing in one direction: forward. Our world is not static. We cannot return to the past, time is the builder of the future. I am convinced that this philosophy is important, not only in its intellectual dimension, but also in relations between individuals and nations. This philosophy should lead us to resolve in a positive manner personal problems as well as the problems of society. In our time one cannot establish a philosophy of life and existence which is not founded on the sciences of nature as they unfold at the present state of knowledge. Humanity is part of nature, a very specific construct of nature on planet earth. During the last fifty years the progress achieved in theoretical physics, in astrophysics, and in cosmology uncovers for us a new image of reality, "ein neues Weltbild," which should guide us in our behavior.

Science, neutral in its essence, is beyond good and evil. Yet it fulfills a very important social function. It leads us to dismantle preconceived ideas and should be instrumental in creating links and bonds between human beings of all cultures.

I have chosen for the greater part of this work the form of a dialogue between Raymond Flammant and myself. Furthermore, the last part will be illustrated by short stories, the very last one long rather than short, because through Omega I want to show what is wrong and could be improved in our society.

Dear Reader, you might think that in this book I am indulging in utopias. But don't let us forget that in the history of mankind the utopias of today are very often the realities of tomorrow.

And now, I wish you stimulating reading.

Part One

Dancing on a Volcano

1. Pampered Child

The Roaring Twenties in Europe

RAYMOND FLAMMANT: When you were born in 1924, Europe was already feeling the impact of the so-called "Roaring Twenties" in the United States. Can this be compared to the literally furious drive to enjoy life in all aspects practically to the last drop of blood in our veins, as featured magnificently in the fifties in the legendary movies with James Dean?

EDMOND ISRAEL: I only know the Roaring Twenties by hearsay, but according to what my parents told me, they were sometimes delirious, excessive in many respects. The young generation, deeply bruised by the First World War, was thirsting to recuperate a youth which had been stolen from it by World War I.

When, for instance, in 1925 a rather difficult period of reconstruction started, our regions were still quite wealthy. This was the time when the people, at least those who could afford it, were literally soaked with pleasure, dancing the Charleston, listening to jazz, but also, listening to the Negro spirituals by the gospel singers. Fashions changed. Women were wearing short dresses above the knee and hats which resembled flower pots turned upside down. They cut their hair short, the so-called "Bubikopf," or in French "la garçonne," a female boy. Evening and night parties lasted to the early hours of the morning, and popular balls and cabarets, particularly in Paris and Berlin, awoke many phantasms in men, to a lesser extent in women. They were signs of freedom in expression, behavior, and attire, sometimes unbridled and without a limit. Preachers and priests called this a new Sodom and Gomorrah. Personally, I rather feel that it was a drive to break the walls made of taboos too often hypocritical in their essence. Yet, it was not the rebellion of the generation of James Dean in the fifties. It was rather an exalted drive to regain lost time.

After all, this generation was not so wrong. Since 1929 the time of dancing, singing, and hunting for pleasure soon came to an end. In October the New York Stock Exchange stumbled and crumbled and the famous "Black Friday" irreversibly drew the world economy into the depression of the thirties.

Just staying for a brief moment with the Roaring Twenties. There was at that time a shining star of the French Music Hall, Josephine Baker. Men were literally thrilled when she appeared on stage: she was sensual, highly attractive, and danced with a G-string of bananas. She received thousands and thousands of love letters and proposals of marriage. You once told me that you met her after the war in a different context here in Luxembourg.

But the Josephine Baker I met personally after the Second World War was a different person. She was by that time already over fifty years old and felt that she had to fulfill the dream of a "universal family." A remarkable idea! She bought some sort of a castle in France and adopted seventy or eighty children of all races, colors and nationalities. At the end of the fifties, she came to Luxembourg following the invitation of the Jewish association,

"B'nai B'rith," the "sons of the Alliance," in order to deliver a multiracial and multiethnic testimony and at the same time collect some funds for her humanitarian activities. I rarely, if ever, have been in the presence of a woman so radiant and charismatic. She was filled to the brim with charm and energy and beaming with sensuality.

Later, her plan met with failure because of financial difficulties. This is a pity because it was an admirable initiative which exemplified an exceptional woman with a noble heart and an ever enticing body. Let me also recall that during the last war under the Nazi occupation in France, she played an important role in the French Resistance movement.

During the Roaring Twenties, how was it in Luxembourg? Was it a bit more calm and quiet than elsewhere?

Sure, and fortunately so. You know, we in Luxembourg are rather balanced and we do not indulge in excesses, neither good ones nor bad ones. In Luxembourg, the "Roaring Twenties" were rather the "Buzzing Twenties."

An annual event of major importance was an international circus, which opened its tents for several weeks in our capital. I remember quite well a rather exceptional attraction. A certain number of pygmies were presented to the public.

In order to attract a maximum number of spectators, the circus paraded the pygmies on the main avenue of Luxembourg City, together with a number of wild animals locked up in cages on wheels, rolling on the pavement of the Avenue de la Liberté. The pygmies danced and rotated their hips to the tunes of African jungle rhythms. For us children, bordering the streets, this was a rare treat and so it was also for the adults. The pygmies appeared as well to be quite happy with the success they met by the enthusiasm of the onlookers.

It was only later that I had a perception of the indecency of this spectacle, which did not appear to shock the people at that time. Human beings were exhibited in the circus in the same manner as exotic animals. I even asked myself to what extent these human beings from Africa were not held overnight in cages or had to sleep on straw like apes and leopards. But I might be a bit unkind and unjust now.

But the Roaring Twenties were not only made of amusement and entertainment. Human endeavor is to reach always higher and faster: for instance, Lindbergh crosses the Atlantic alone in plane for the first time in 1927. Two mountain climbers, Mallory and Irvine, died close to the summit of Mount Everest. By the way, it's not known whether they have reached the summit as did Edmund Hillary some twenty-five years later.

But don't forget science: Einstein, Hubble, Bohr, Heisenberg, relativity and quantum mechanics. Keynes published his first works on economics. Broadcasting started to completely change the process of disseminating information.

And then there are the painters like Kandinsky, Kokoschka, Klee, Münch, Chagall, Picasso, Miro, just to mention a few who come to my mind spontaneously, and in music, the everlasting "Rhapsody in Blue" by Gershwin. In the movies, the admirable achievements of Charlie Chaplin and Eisenstein. In literature Thomas Mann publishes *The Magic Mountain* (*Der Zauberberg*). Tucholsky, Kästner, and Gide are very fashionable. And this reminds me of the literary encounters organized at the castle in Colpach, Luxembourg, by the wife of Emile Mayrisch, Aline de Saint-Hubert, where André Gide was a frequent visitor. Mies van der Rohe and Le Corbusier started to revolutionize architecture.

I am always astonished at the artistic creation of the Twenties. I often asked myself how a period as creative as the one I just mentioned was gradually engulfing itself in the blackest of all human tragedies, the Holocaust, the final milestone on the road of horror and abomination. I still have not found an answer to my question.

Coming back to artistic creation, you once told me that as a small child, when you were three years old, and were not able to write, you scribbled on paper letters intended for an imaginary person. These scribbled notes had been detected by your mother when she was cleaning the floor under the rugs where you were hiding these notes.

Yes, this is true. I still have a vague memory of this. I even gave a name to the recipient of my notes. I called him "Geili" and I mentally developed some kind of a relationship with him, but that's long, long ago.

Good old Sigmund Freud would probably enjoy this story.

Oh, you know, psychoanalysis never interested me very much. For me, the human being primarily constructs himself and evolves in relationship with his environment and the knowledge he acquires. Instincts are a part of the animal nature present in us. They are the medium for pleasure and procreation, and that's basically all. Furthermore, the conscious state interests me more than the sub-conscious. I never felt the necessity to indulge into speleological exercises in my innermost, my sub-consciousness, or to spend years on a sofa telling a specialist my phantasms, my dreams or what passes or appears to pass through my mind, in short, what is apparently hidden in me and must get out so that I can heal.

What fascinates me is to live, to live intensely, to construct, to be oriented and targeted to the future. Is it a personal therapy? I don't know. Am I a neurotic or a psychopath who ignores his psychic ailments? Perhaps! But this is of no interest for me. Let me here recall the famous phrase of Dr. Knock: "We are all sick, but we just don't know it."

Let me come back to my taste for writing. I also wrote poems as a child. When I was ten or twelve years old, my mother and I were passing our vacation in Arosa, Switzerland because I had to avoid chronic bronchitis. It was the first time I saw high mountains. I marveled at the sight and I expressed my wonderment and awe through probably completely worthless poems. After our return, my father felt strongly that he was the fortunate genitor of a precocious poet, and possibly of a genius. He put my poems into an envelope and sent them to his brother-in-law, my uncle Max, who lived in Berlin. And in an accompanying letter he gave free course to his enthusiasm and described what he considered an exceptional event, the making of a poet. Every day my father anxiously awaited the mail and a reply from Uncle Max. He imagined that perhaps his brother-in-law was already looking for an editor. But no letter arrived and finally uncle Max sent him a brief note, which my father read in silence and then put aside. The whole family, including my aunt Clementine and my uncle David, understood that the comments of Uncle Max were not too complimentary. By the way, neither I nor any member of the family ever found out what Uncle Max thought of my first works of art.

I hope that this did not create a deep rift in your family?

Certainly not. Our family was tightly knit together. It took my father some time until he got over it. At the next visit of Uncle Max to Luxembourg, there was some explaining and reconciliation. Later on, they laughed and amused themselves by evoking this event.

Cocooning in the family fold

You mentioned your parents, your uncles, and aunts. I think the moment has come to speak about them. You grew up in a family which was rather like a tribe, a clan. As a child you must have been in the center of this family. You were coddled, pampered, and spoiled. Is that right?

Yes of course, especially as far as my parents, my uncle David, and my aunt Clementine are concerned. We all lived in one household, in one apartment and I was the only child of the family, as Uncle David and Aunt Clementine were childless. But they all brought me up, and they gave me a lot of affection, I would even say a super dose of love and kindness. This is the main source from which I derived throughout my life the necessary energy to confront many challenges and dangers.

Let me now give you a brief description of the four. On my father's side, the ancestors were of the Lorraine, the French region bordering Luxembourg. As a vagrant of history, the region of Lorraine was sometimes German, sometimes French. My ancestors felt very French. There were Francophiles, particularly my grand-mother, Jeannette. My great-great-grandparents left the Lorraine around 1810 for Luxembourg, in the wake of the French Revolution, which granted to the Jews the same civil rights enjoyed by the other members of society. As my inclination is more to anticipate and construct the future than to indulge in the past, I never made any genealogical research about my ancestors. My father was born in the Rue St.-Ulrich in the "Grund," a suburb of Luxembourg. His parents were of a very modest condition. They had a small textile business. All this has been told to me by my father, because I never had the good fortune to know my grandparents on both sides.

My grandfather apparently was quite a character. He was a striking example of an autodidact, as he had practically no schooling. He had a natural intelligence and I inherited from him both my taste for self-education, a kind of lifelong learning, as well as some sort of selective anxiety. I have been told that my grandfather was terribly afraid of thunderstorms, but he obstinately refused to go to a shelter when during the First World War, Luxembourg City and in particular the sector where he lived, was bombed.

My father, Gustave Israel, fourth generation in Luxembourg was also born in the suburb, in the "Grund," which at present has become a very fashionable part of the city of Luxembourg, with its cultural establishments, its museums and its attraction to the younger people in a number of "bistros" and side-walk "cafés." At the time when my father was born, the "Grund" was a poor, drab part of Luxembourg City shunned by the upper and middle class, called the *haute bourgeoisie* and the *bourgeoisie*. As a matter of fact, some people spent their childhood in the Grund and upgraded their social status when they were able to afford to live in the upper part of the city without ever referring to their birth place. In our family, this has never been the case. For instance, I am proud to recall the time when I was a factory worker in the U.S.A. In this respect, as in many other aspects, I feel very American.

But let's come back to my parents. My father met my mother through an encounter arranged by the rabbi of Luxembourg in 1921. As a matter of fact, my father and his sister, Clementine met my mother and her brother David at the same time.

My father was enthusiastic when he first saw my mother, who was a beauty, a very quiet and cultured person. After the first meeting he asked her to marry him. He put one condition: that her brother would marry his sister. My mother was slightly amused, and said "Be patient, patience is a virtue." But in a relatively short period of time the four concluded that they would create a family. My mother married my father and her brother married the sister of my father on the same day at the former synagogue in Luxembourg. That synagogue was later destroyed during the last World War by the Nazis, when they occupied and incorporated the Grand-Duchy of Luxembourg into the Third Reich. Let me add here that my mother and her brother, David Lande, had been born in a small village called Feuerstein, not far from Lissa in the province of Posen (or Poznan in Polish). This border region between Germany and Poland was alternatively Polish and German (just like the Lorraine was at times German and at times French). When my mother was born, the province of Posen was German. After the First World War, it became Polish.

Without going into too many details, let me just point out that my father was an autodidact, much attracted by philosophy. Professionally, he was conscientious and like his father and now me, he was selectively anxious. For instance, he worked as manager of a large furniture store six days a week, sometimes even on Sunday mornings. Very trusted by his employer, he had a key to the safe in the office of the store where valuables and cash were deposited. Quite often, my father, on Sunday afternoon, suddenly had a feeling of anxiety. He would then run to the store to check whether he had locked the safety vault. As far as I can recollect, it was never left open but he wanted to be sure.

My mother on her side, was an intelligent, quiet woman, and as I said before, a striking beauty. Contrary to my father who was very extroverted, she was a trifle introverted. Sometimes she quoted a phrase from a German novel "Lerne leiden, ohne zu klagen," *You must learn how to suffer without complaining.* She had this natural dignity never to complain. It was a great lesson for me and I followed this precept throughout all my life. It is better to rouse envy than pity. The two couples rented an apartment in a rather old and not very comfortable house situated not far from the Luxembourg train station, yet no longer in the suburb where my father and his sister were born. The apartment consisted of two bedrooms, a kitchen with an old stove, and a living room. There was at that time no electricity in the apartment, only gaslight. And of course central heating was just a dream.

Quite a number of women did not go to the obstetric clinic to give birth to their child. My mother followed this example and so I came to the world at home, probably in the bedroom of my parents. The obstetrician having been on vacation when I was born, it was a midwife, apparently a very capable one, who assisted my mother in her labors. I sometimes met the midwife, a very homely and corpulent woman with wide breasts bulging with nourishing milk, in the streets of Luxembourg. Then she never failed to shout with her stentorian voice "Oh, here is the sweet little boy who was dead when he came to the world! I plunged him alternatively into hot and icy water and then suddenly the first cry came out of his mouth and from the inner-most of his lungs." She reveled at evoking this event.

Reflecting on this, I still have a little pang in my heart. Coming to life, entering the stage of the human comedy is both a miracle and a coincidence. Indeed it takes so little and it won't happen.

So your uncle David and aunt Clementine never had children.

Unfortunately not. I say unfortunately because it is a tragedy for a couple not to give birth to a child. I know that out of my personal experience.

Under one single roof, in one household there were two women, one of them having a child and the other one, not. Even though the two couples felt very close to each other, this situation sometimes created strains and stress. My mother silently suffered from this situation but according to her principle she never complained. As a matter of fact, as far as I can remember, she never said anything which could have disrupted the harmony of the family. My aunt was of course frustrated; she was an extrovert, quite different from my mother, but in her heart she was a very good person. As a child I enjoyed the fact that I received attention and love from two women and from two men. I had two mothers and two fathers. In every human being there is quite a dose of egoism and in children, it is more apparent. Only later, I was dimly aware of what my mother sometimes had to support. But, and this is very important, the four of them gave me a lot of affection and love.

Did it occur to you in one or the other phases of your life that perhaps in your upbringing you had not been sufficiently prepared for the rough and tough moments in a human existence and that the education which was given to you was too soft?

Later in my life I recognized this. Some of the bruises of my soul, bruises which the French author, Françoise Sagan, calls "*les bleus à l'âme*" would not have been so painful if my education had been different. But what was important was the love, the affection, and the warmth I received as well as the solidarity and harmony in our family. This, I believe, allowed me to weather successfully many storms, many difficulties in my own existence. The treasure of love is what makes life livable, developing in many people a passion for life.

Just two examples of how concerned my father was:

In summer, in spite of his high professional conscience, he sometimes slid away from the store to rush to the municipal park where my mother was promenading me in a baby carriage, just to find out whether the child was sufficiently covered in order not to catch cold.

Before my entrance to the primary school there was a family council, as a matter of fact many councils, and on the particular insistence of my father, the family unanimously decided to move nearer to my school so that I did not have to walk too far. Where we lived it was about a five minutes walk to my school. But they all moved to an apartment just across the street from the school. It is difficult to realize today that four adults changed their apartment, implying expenses and all the unpleasantry of moving from one place to another, just for the sake of more comfort and security of their common child. It was an irrational decision and at the same time an act of solicitude and love.

In the context of my childhood years, let me add that my father, who had a passion for literature and philosophy, tried, when I was six or seven years old, to convey to me the beauty of poetry, particularly of Goethe, whose works he admired above all. He also patiently explained to me the basic thoughts of Kant, Schopenhauer, and Leibniz. I of course did not understand anything. But he succeeded in awakening in me as early as possible a taste, if not a passion for philosophy, for the search for a meaning of our existence as well as of the universe of which we are part.

I also recall with delight the school free Tuesday and Thursday afternoons I spent in the pastry stores of many towns of Luxembourg, when I was allowed to accompany my uncle David, who was a traveling salesman. While he visited his customers, small or medium-sized textile stores, I ravenously devoured apple pies, cheese pies, chocolate cakes with vanilla coatings and lots of whipped cream. I must confess that throughout all my life I continue to crave philosophy and sweet pastries. But as in my later years, I have become a weight watcher, and pastry ranks more and more in the category of unfulfilled desires. This is also the case in my search to unlock the mystery of the Universe.

School and self-education

You have not yet spoken of your schooling. You probably forgot it.

Let's say that my years at school have not left me with a lasting impression.

It appears that I was a rather gifted pupil and student. At least that's what my respectable teacher at primary school, Mr. Medernach, communicated. He encouraged my father to let me pursue my studies at high school as well as at the university. He predicted to him a brilliant future for me, more specifically as a university professor. I think that, in this respect, my father did not need any convincing.

Fate decided a different direction for me. In the end, school has only played a secondary role in my life. My studies at the

Luxembourg High School, Athénée de Luxembourg, were inter-rupted by the invasion of our country by the Nazis in May 1940. After the war, I successfully passed the final high school exam, called in Luxembourg "baccalauréat," thanks to an accelerated process and a number of facilities granted to the boys who had been drafted by the Nazi occupier as well as those who were of Jewish faith and had to leave the country.

After the war, I had to decide whether to pursue my studies in a University. I was not particularly drawn to that, first, because my father was ill and I had to earn a living for me and the family. But today, I think that they could have coped with that and would have been willing to make sacrifices for me as they did all their life. A more profound reason is the fact that disciplined learning, which I probably wrongly perceived and still perceive in retrospect as more descriptive then prospective, does not corre-spond to my mindset, endowed with an irrepressible imagination pulling me into multidirectional mental peregrinations. Some rather painful experiences at school confirmed this attitude in me. I recall that I was not too good in arithmetic. That's why I probably became a banker. Not successfully finding a solution to a problem, I was called to the blackboard by a rather primitive teacher who hammered my head at the blackboard, each hit a phase in the process towards the solution of the problem. This experience left a ripple on my soul alongside the many bruises, which I already mentioned before.

I was a fat child and my physical condition did not allow me to practice sport or even to participate in the games requiring a certain physical fitness and agility. Added to that, my parents decided, when I was six years old, that for the first year a teacher should give me private lessons so that I did not need to be exposed to the constraints and disciplines of a school. Added to that they were afraid that I could catch an infectious disease presenting great risks in view of my fragile health. So after the first twelve months of private lessons, I started at school and I was immediately considered an outsider. I developed a natural timidity as well as a great sensitivity at being mocked. The French poet La Fontaine said, speaking of children, "*cet âge ne connaît pas de pitié*," this generation has no pity. If he lived today, he would have extended this statement to all ages, but that's not the point.

Do you think that being scoffed at and mocked at was at least partly due to the fact that you were a Jew?

I don't know. As a matter of fact I don't think so. At the time of my childhood the different religious communities, of which the Catholic one was by far the most important, lived in separate spheres. I never experienced any aggressive or violent anti-Semitism. Not at that time, and certainly not today, and that's to the honor of Luxembourg, which is a country of immigration. For a number of reasons, mainly economic ones, we accept people immigrating to Luxembourg without too many difficulties. We had a major influx of Italians at the beginning of the twentieth century, and in the midst of the twentieth century, around 1960, a new wave of immigrants from Portugal entered our country. At the present time, more than eighteen percent of the Luxembourg population are Portuguese or of Portuguese origin. They keep their cultural traditions but at the same time integrate in the social and cultural fabric of Luxembourg. This is true, particularly for the younger generation. As far as the Jewish segment of the Luxembourg society is concerned, the painful experiences suffered both by Gentiles and Jews during the last World War, created new and very strong bonds of solidarity and even friendship between the two components of our population.

Beyond the pleasant and nourishing moments you passed in pastry stores, thanks to your uncle David, how did you spend your leisure time?

I liked to read. I devoured books. Particularly those of Erich Kästner, a German author who wrote detective stories for children like *Emil und die Detektive* (*Emil and the Detectives*), *Das fliegende Klassenzimmer* (*The Flying Schoolroom*), and *Pünktchen und Anton*. At the same time I was fascinated by the adventure stories of another German author, Karl May. He situated his novels both in the far west of the United States and in Middle Eastern countries. He wrote with an astonishing imagination, because apparently he never set foot in these regions. Some of his heroes remain vivid in my memory, like Old Surehand, Old Shatterhand, Kara ben Nemsi, Winnetou, Sam the Trapper, and a colorful figure, he called Hadschi Halef Omar Ben Hadschi Abdul Abbas Ibn Hadschi Dawud al Gossara. They were real persons for me and sometimes I thought that I would meet them around the corner of the Rue de Strasbourg where we lived.

And then there was the passionate initiation into philosophy by my father.

After school, I also liked to accompany my mother and my aunt to a coffee shop, a "Kaffeehaus," called "Paris Palace." There was a pianist, a violinist, and a cellist interpreting melodies of that time. I listened to them in silence and my thoughts were migrating to imaginary worlds. I sometimes sat at another table, alone by myself, because the conversations of my mother and my aunt with friends were boring me and alone I prepared my lessons for the next day. I still very much like this atmosphere, which is particularly characteristic of Vienna and Prague. When I am in these towns, I am very fond of having a cup of coffee in a "Kaffeehaus" and I imagine that Kafka or Max Brod or Stefan Zweig will open the door, sit down at a table, sip an espresso, and write the novels which are an important part of the European literary heritage.

Let's come back to your studies. After primary school it's high school, isn't it?

Yes, I was admitted at the Athénée of Luxembourg and I signed myself up for the Latin session. One of the immediate consequences was that my parents, aunt, and uncle moved again from the Rue de Strasbourg to the Rue Adolphe Fisher, where my father had bought a house, which was nearer to the Athénée.

Competition in the Latin section was quite keen. I love languages and I have a particularly fond memory of my Latin teacher, Ernest Ludovicy. He was very adept at motivating students and he explained to us that Latin is an unequalled mental exercise to learn how to think clearly and logically. He continued in his praise of Latin, stressing that it helps you to understand and learn foreign languages. Ernest Ludovicy was a timid man, but he had a great heart and a high sense of justice. When we were refugees in France and I wrote to him to get a certificate of scholarship, he went to see the Nazi director of the Athénée, who shouted at him, "Why do you want to help this dirty Jew?" Since Ernest Ludovicy insisted, he obtained the certificate and sent it to me. This was quite daring, very courageous of a man who gave the impression of being shy and timorous.

We met again after the war and founded an interconfessional committee which soon was transformed into an association. For the first time in Luxembourg, dating back to 1965, we co-organized a Jewish-Christian public conference. The speakers were the Reverend Father Riquet, well-known as an eminent member of the French Resistance movement and a preacher of Notre Dame in Paris, a Protestant pastor, Mr. Lacoque, as well as the chief rabbi of Luxembourg, Emmanuel Bulz. The topic was the man of today and his attitude toward God. The three speakers dealt with this topic in the light of their own religion. This event drew a large crowd. The younger people were especially interested and there were not sufficient seats in the conference room of the Casino of Luxembourg which normally seats three hundred persons. Thus the younger people were sitting on the floor. This was a very encouraging sign for all of us for our future activity.

I could imagine that the question of if there is God after Auschwitz, occupied an important part of the debates.

Naturally. It is a difficult and painful question.

And what was the conclusion? And if I may also ask, what is your personal reply to that question?

I shall come back more in detail to this later, in the course of our conversation. Let me just say in the context of our present conversation that God or the transcendental reality, is timeless but that the way of speaking about God is changing in time.

You were brought up in a religious and practicing family conscientiously following the precepts of Moses. Does this religious education leave you with many memories?

Of course, quite a number. My religious upbringing constitutes an important part of my education. I remember very well the first time my parents brought me to the synagogue. I was impressed by the chief rabbi on the altar (at that time it was Robert Serebrenick) and I looked continuously at him. At the end of the ceremony, he shook hands with each and every one of the members attending the service and then he gently stroked my cheeks and in a firm voice said: "You were not too noisy, that's good. But the next time, don't stare so much at my face, but rather look into your prayer book."

A more lasting memory goes back to the celebration of my Bar-Mitzvah which, in the Jewish religion, is the day when a boy reaches the age of thirteen years, and therefore of maturity, becoming a full-fledged member of the community. My Bar-Mitzvah was celebrated in 1937. According to the prescriptions, I was called to the altar to read an excerpt of the Torah, which in Judaism is the book of learning, of wisdom and ethics given by

God to Moses on Mount Sinai. Every Saturday morning, a small part of the Torah written on parchment scrolls is recited by the Chasan, the cantor, and on his Bar-Mitzvah, the boy takes the place of the cantor for some minutes by reading aloud these excerpts written without vowels. This makes the reading quite difficult. The recitation has to be made in a specific melody; each syllable has its own intonation from which one is not allowed to deviate. I prepared for this exercise six months before and my parents transported a piano to our house where the cantor instilled into me each intonation. It's one of those memories I don't like to be reminded of, because I was not particularly gifted at reading from the Torah with the right intonation. Anyhow, according to what my family and my friends told me, my performance was not too bad. Of course my father and uncle thought it was of the highest quality.

In the evening, the family and friends assembled for dinner at a boarding house, or let's call it a "restaurant" which was situated in the lower part of the city of Luxembourg. This restaurant most definitely had no star in the Michelin, but instead it had a label of "kosher," which means only food in accordance with the Jewish prescriptions is served there. The quality of the dinner, as far as I can remember, was quite good. It was a menu in the Jewish tradition: the Jewish fish, carp, then chicken broth with dumplings as well as goose with all the traditional stuffing and trimmings filled the plates up to the brim. At that time, nobody paid attention to the number of calories but our stomachs certainly had to work overtime on that evening.

On the intellectual side, my father had hired a literary entertainer. He was a well-known German writer of short stories and gave brilliant performances on the stages of literary cabarets in the Berlin of the pre-Nazi period. His name was Karl Schnog, and in my view he ranked very high in the category of the German so-called "Feuilletonists" such as Heinrich Heine, Kurt Tucholsky, and Erich Kästner. Karl Schnog was a German blend of Mark Twain and Bernard Shaw. He had to flee Nazi Germany because he was very outspoken in his humorous remarks against the Nazi dictator. Wit and peppered humor are the sworn enemies of Nazis and fascists, in particular if the author is Jewish. Therefore, he risked the concentration camp, even death, if he had stayed in Germany. So, as a refugee, he was hired to bring fun and amusement at family gatherings. Later in my life I realized how tragic this was for such a talented and brilliant man.

The family of the youngest brother of my mother, Alex, who lived in Breslau, Germany, also attended the Bar-Mitzvah celebration, along with his wife, my aunt Margot, and her daughter Eva, who was six years old.

My father suggested to them, in fact to my mother's whole family still living in Germany, that they come and establish themselves in Luxembourg. This was one more testimony of my father's generosity. But the German family knew better. They suffered the trials and vexations of the Nazi persecution, which, as known today, led to the Holocaust. For them Luxembourg was too near to Germany. Not only did they refuse to establish themselves in a more permanent manner in Luxembourg, but they also strongly advised my father and his family to leave Luxembourg. If their advice had been followed, we would have been spared from many tribulations and dangers and my life would certainly have taken a different turn.

Before evoking the ordeals, you went through during the war, let us now close the chapter of your educational itinerary.

I don't know really what to add. My schooling ended abruptly on May 10, 1940, the date of the German invasion. When I left the Athénée on the afternoon of May 9, I had of course not the slightest inkling that this was my last day at this school. In the evening I went to bed neither more nor less worried than the other days. Waking up in the morning, everything had changed.

And you were becoming an autodidact like your father . . .

Indeed, most of the things I know, I learned by myself. As time goes on and now, at the dusk of my life I realize more and more how much I am a replica of my father. First, physically when I look at some of his photographs, I see myself in these pictures. He has also transmitted to me a certain dose of professional conscientiousness, and above all, his taste for philosophy and also his anxieties. Just like my father, I select my anxieties. I am strong and calm in front of great dangers and I worry a lot for matters which are rather futile and do not constitute the slightest cause for concern. Later in my professional life, when I was confronted with a really serious problem, I kept my composure and usually asked my collaborators to describe to me in a few words the worst case scenario. And then I set myself to devise an appropriate solution and took a decision. Another proof of my selective anxiety: I never hesitated to take a plane to regions presenting some dangers. On the other side, I am terribly tense when I have to take a blood test until I get the results.

In Luxembourg the laboratories work very fast and it takes them twenty-four hours to deliver the results. Waiting for them, usually in the afternoon, when the clock shows 3 P.M., my nervous system takes the form of a violin on which the strings are too tight. And at each moment, I risk a nervous breakdown. This was also the cause in 2001, when I had a very bad fall while rushing down from my office to the fax machine to check whether my blood results had been sent. I tripped, missed a step, and fell down the wooden stairs from the second to the first floor. Blood was running all over my face, my head had a large wound, and my neck was completely out of place. It took me three months to be presentable again. I still suffer from this fall and regularly need special treatment by a physical therapist. Later at the hospital, where I was transported by an ambulance, my first question was "How is my blood test?" The nurses were amused, the doctor had a smile on his face and he answered "In this respect, no worry! You better take care of your spine and neck." He could have put it in a different manner, but that is another chapter to which perhaps one day I shall refer in a short story which could be entitled "The Doctor and the Anxious Patient."

Let's get back to your question.

As an autodidact, you may have noticed that I follow to a great extent the trend of our time by practicing lifelong learning.

In this line of thinking would you recommend to young people today to follow your example of self-education?

Really not. It's a very difficult road. Whatever one's talent and gift, one is disadvantaged with regard to those who have completed higher education with one or several diplomas.

The principles of lifelong learning should, however, reset the scales in favor of the autodidact who practices this system right from the start. Perhaps, but I am not so sure of this, the autodidacts are a bit more creative by not being burdened by lots of details and technicalities taught in schools.

The first signs of a devastating blaze

Reviewing the years from your birth until the end of the twenties, one has the impression that everything is for the best in the best of worlds. Fun and pleasure instead of blood and battlefields. On the major stock exchanges, particularly on Wall Street, prices keep on soaring. Markets were basking in the sun of "irrational exuberance," a definition coined by Alan Greenspan, for the market's behavior in the late nineties. Was it so really?

I couldn't tell out of experience because I was too young at that time. Yet, if I peruse newspapers, magazines, or books, what you just said appears to me quite correct. Mankind was dancing on a volcano which rumbled but did not yet burst into flames, sputtering its hot lava down its slopes. The rumbling volcano induced far-sighted and visionary politicians like Coudenhove-Kalergy to call even at that time for a United Europe. The president of the United States, Woodrow Wilson, perhaps too idealistic to be followed, proposed the creation of a League of Nations on a worldwide scale, a premature initiative which only many years later, after the "blood and toil and tears" of the Second World War, became a reality with the creation of the United Nations.

In Italy, fascism was in power since 1922, under Benito Mussolini. Hitler, after he failed to gain power in 1924, and after having completed his book *Mein Kampf* in 1926, finally succeeded to become chancellor of the "Reich" in 1933. This was the start of a reign which caused not only the Second World War, but also the Holocaust, an unprecedented genocide in recorded human history.

Yet already in the thirties, from time to time some ripples on the flat ocean of optimistic complacency awoke feelings of anxiety. After Hitler came into power and in his strident hysteric voice proclaimed a policy of Blood and Soil, "Blut und Boden," it appears strange to me that the principle democratic powers were not reacting directly and did not see the danger which was looming on the horizon, soon engulfing practically the whole world.

Yes, it was some kind of blindness. The great nations were led by politicians, who desperately tried to find ways and means to compose with the paranoiac of Berchtesgaden. You know I am not a historian, therefore I am not competent to analyze the causes which led Hitler to seize power leading to the Second World War. Some people mention as a major cause the failure of the democracies, too weak and inconsistent to cope effectively with the threats. Others said that Germany was humiliated and confronted with a major economic crisis leading to a staggering inflation and high figures of unemployment. In that nation, hunger prevailed and when Hitler came into power he created jobs with the assistance of the German "War Lords." Some were powerful "steel makers," others bankers. They all earned a lot of money and thus let Hitler pursue his goals of murder and devastation. There is a thought, coming to my mind or rather a statement made frequently: "History repeats itself." My own personal philosophy does not accept this: "Nothing is permanent but change." So history does not repeat itself but sometimes political leaders, when confronted by great dangers, take similar positions. Lacking a better definition, I would call this phenomenon the "Chamberlain-Daladier effect."

Let us, for a moment, jump over seventy years. Today we are confronted with the worldwide threat of terrorism. One can make subtle analyses of the causes of terrorism. The fact is that a major catastrophe can hardly be avoided if the democracies continue to turn a blind eye to this threat and even attempt some sort of appeasement and compromise with those who want to enslave the civilized world, who are driven by many forces, such as the search of power and wealth, or the fanatical belief that they act in the name of God. Instead of cooperating and coordinating their efforts on a worldwide scale, some nations follow the policy of Chamberlain and Daladier. But this, my dear friend, would be the topic of another book.

Yes, let's come back to Luxembourg. Have you some recollections of the period of time preceding the invasion of Luxembourg on May 10, 1940?

Not many as far as the overall political and economic situation in our country are concerned. Of course, the progressive deterioration of the economy on an international scale did not leave Luxembourg unscathed. As our economy was based primarily on steel and iron, ARBED, the most representative company in this sector, was continuously laying off people and so this had a negative impact on the overall situation.

How was life in your family?

My father had a rather comfortable professional situation as manager of a flourishing furniture store. Financially, we were not affected much. In my family, existence continued with all the features of a Luxembourg middle-class family of Jewish faith. We scrupulously respected the dietary laws of Moses. Only "kosher" meat was on the table. Pork and ham were just abominations. In a family like ours, the main meal consisted of meat or fish with lots of potatoes, some vegetables, and bread. My mother and aunt bought the fish in the open air market, not in specialized seafood stores or supermarkets like today. Like many women, they examined the ears of the fish in order to find out whether it was fresh. As already mentioned, our apartment had no electricity and was lighted through candles and gas. The streets were also lit by gas. My mother and aunt washed their linen in cauldrons in the cellar. I sometimes went down to watch the proceedings, but I did not like the smell which came out of the cauldrons. The dirty linen was washed in boiling water mixed with some sort of soap powder. It was a strenuous physical effort for the women. I watched and did not help because I have a propensity to be a passive onlooker when physical efforts are involved.

Leaving your family a moment, from what point in time did people in Luxembourg become seriously concerned with the danger which could lead to war?

After the invasion of Czechoslovakia and the incorporation of Austria in the German Reich, anxiety grew at an increasingly fast pace. However, hope still prevailed that the worst could be avoided. And even the Jews, though they were threatened by Hitler to be erased from the face of the earth, had the hope that Daladier and Chamberlain could bring Hitler to reason. In Luxembourg, anxiety permeated all strata of society and some sort of solidarity emerged in the face of the common danger. The government still tried very hard to appease the dictator across the border, believing that the traditional neutrality of Luxembourg could be preserved even in the case of war. Bolshevism in the communist Soviet Union was considered by many as the greater threat and this was so until the so-called non-aggression pact signed by Hitler and Stalin, a pact which came to an end when Germany invaded the Soviet Union in 1941.

In 1939 Luxembourg celebrated with great pomp and festive parades the hundredth anniversary of its independence. This was obviously a manifestation of self-delusion. In reality neither great parades nor appeasing statements could restrain the Nazis across the border from invading Luxembourg, if this proved a necessity in the strategy devised by a pathological mind such as the one of Adolph Hitler. The facts proved a few months later that this indeed was the case.

The dilemma: die or die in trickles?

What was the situation like at this critical period time for the Jewish community as well as the majority of Luxembourgers of Catholic faith? But first, what about anti-Semitism in our country? Was it a serious problem?

I can only refer to my own experience. Anti-Semitism in Luxembourg was not a dominant feature. In essence anti-Semitism and racism are diseases for which conclusive remedies have not yet been discovered. AIDS is an organic disease; racism and anti-Semitism are mental illnesses. If the conditions, preventing the outbreak of these diseases are not met, then they have the tendency to spread like wildfire on barren land. In both cases preventive measures have to be taken. As far as the mental diseases, racism and anti-Semitism, are concerned, I think that in our time it needs "new thinking" to be implanted in the minds of people, even in their childhood. This new thinking, which I will elaborate more amply later in our conversation, calls for the dismantling of preconceived ideas, for recognizing the dignity of the other, regardless of his creed and culture. At the same time sound social and economic conditions are essential to avoid the outbreak of racism and anti-Semitism. Let me repeat that in Luxembourg, perhaps because of the size of the country and the mentality of its people, anti-Semitism was never a dominant feature in the fabric of the society. Furthermore, the common threat of Nazism affecting all the Luxembourgers of all creeds and traditions, whether Catholics or Jews, gradually became a binding factor between the various religions.

In the thirties, Luxembourg, like most of the Western European countries, felt a dual danger, the first one coming from the Soviet Union, defined as Bolshevism, the other one from Germany, Nazism. That was the time when the governments of the Western European democracies thought that there was a possibility to co-exist with the dictator in Berlin. Perhaps some people of great influence thought that Nazism after all was the lesser evil, as compared to Bolshevism. Such people existed in many countries including Luxembourg. For the Jews, however, there was no choice: their sworn enemy was Nazism, which systematically fulfilled the plan of Adolf Hitler to eradicate the Jews from this planet. The establishment of the first concentration camps of Dachau and Buchenwald as well as the "Reichkristallnacht" of 1938, when practically all the synagogues in Germany were burnt and demolished, were threatening signals of doom and death for the Jews.

Therefore, the time approached for us when we had to prepare ourselves to leave our country if the worst should happen. We were strengthened in this attitude when the Second World War broke out in September 1939. On a more personal note, both my uncles Alex and Max in Germany who felt the danger in their very own existence, never ceased to admonish us to leave the country and to take refuge in places at a reasonably safe distance from Luxembourg.

Uncle Max lived in Berlin. He was an industrialist, quite successful in his business and a respected member of the Berlin society. Like a number of German Jews, he thought that when Hitler came to power, somehow things would work out, that a democracy like Germany, a nation which produced the most brilliant representatives in culture, in literature, in science could not maintain in power the brutal and primitive bunch of criminals like the Nazis. But he was wrong. He was married to my aunt Alice, who came from a Protestant German family. After the racial laws of Nürenberg prohibited under the threat of jail and even death the marriage between what the Germans called pure Aryans and Jews, he was condemned to a prison sentence, because of "Rassenschande" (shameless violation of racial laws). Thanks to some connections and a costly lawyer, he was freed from prison and immediately left Germany. His wife preceded him and took a job with an English family in London as governess. Both established themselves in Brussels where they stayed until the invasion of Belgium. On May 10, 1940 they fled to the South of France.

My uncle Alex and his family left Germany in 1938, passing through Luxembourg and then going to South America, Chile. My uncle Alex had fought gallantly in the German army during the First World War. He even received the Iron Cross, second-class, for acts of courage and bravery. In a tramway in Breslau where he had a haberdashery store, he was insulted by a Nazi. He got up and vigorously slapped the face of this Nazi on both cheeks. Afterwards, it was too dangerous for him to stay and fortunately he and his family were able to leave in time.

All this, as well as the increasingly disquieting news coming from across the border, induced us to make the necessary preparation to leave Luxembourg. As a youngster at that time, fourteen or fifteen years old, I was particularly insistent in this respect. I listened to the speeches of Adolf Hitler on the radio and I was convinced that he would consistently and relentlessly execute his plan to kill all the Jews. I thought that it was essential to go on living and not to be killed prematurely. I was young and even for the older people, I think, it was worthwhile going on living. It was just as simple and fundamental as that, and so I kept on insisting and even harassing my parents, my uncle, and aunt not to hesitate, not to wait too long. My mother was in complete agreement with me in her own way. Quietly but persistently she kept telling my father that we had to leave Luxembourg as soon as possible, that there was no alternative. My father devised plans for departing from Luxembourg once the worst would happen, but while staying in Luxembourg he hoped that somehow things would not turn out as badly as feared. He was not the only one thinking like this. Many Jews in Luxembourg and all over Europe had a similar view. They were basking in illusions. That is a human feature. We find such attitudes practically throughout all the recorded history of mankind. Even today in the twenty-first century, many people feel that the United States is overreacting in its fight against terrorism, that the dialogue should be pursued with the so-called rogue nations, that in the last resort those nations fomenting terrorism could be partners in a constructive dialogue with democracies. This is what I call, and I repeat myself, the "Chamberlain-Daladier" effect.

The "Arlon" plan

But let us return to Luxembourg and to preparations made by my own family. My father was convinced that if the war broke out and France was attacked, the Maginot Line, an iron wall along the main borders between France and Germany, would hold and would repel the German invaders. Thus, my parents rented a small apartment in Arlon, a town situated in Belgium, across the border of Luxembourg. We even bought a used car, model 1920, which was placed in a garage in a suburb of Luxembourg and my father had an agreement with a driver to bring us across the border to Belgium whenever needed. Indeed, neither my father nor my uncle had a driver's license. My father strangely believed that Belgium would be spared, even if Luxembourg were invaded. After the pounding from the French Maginot Line, under the command of General Gamelin, the Germans would retreat and would be defeated within a very short period of time, possibly after several weeks. Then we could return to Luxembourg. That was, to quote the title of a famous French movie picture "La grande illusion," *The Great Illusion*. I understand my father now more than in the past. He painfully constructed a career which he did not want to abandon. This illusion was shared by many Jews in Luxembourg, by many people all over Europe.

This situation of the state of hazy uncertainty prevailed until May 10, 1940, when my father early in the morning received a call from a friend living in a bordering town between Germany and Luxembourg: "D'Preisen sin do!" *The Germans are here!*

Part Two

SURVIVING, LIVING, CONSTRUCTING

2. Refugee

The Rescue Operation "Arlon"

The tenth of May 1940 marked the end of the so-called "Funny War," "la Drôle de guerre," which started with the invasion of Poland by Germany in September 1939. France and England had declared war but did not make it. In Europe, the real hostilities began only after May 10, 1940, the day Hitler had chosen to attack France. To general surprise he did not launch a frontal attack across the border against the Maginot Line, which he circumvented by invading Luxembourg, Belgium, and the Netherlands.

As mentioned before, your family had been warned through the telephone call by a friend of your father.

Indeed, we had had the telephone installed in our apartment. Owning a telephone was at that time rather a luxury but essential for emergencies. The call reached us at five in the morning of the tenth of May 1940. A few minutes later we received a call from the son-in-law of my father's boss, owner of the furniture store. They did not live far from our apartment. He said: "Get ready in twenty minutes. I'll come and fetch you. If you are not in the street at that time, I shall drive on. I am a French officer and therefore in danger if I fall into the hands of the Germans."

From that moment on we realized that we had to leave in haste, not even washing ourselves, hardly taking any clothes, tossing some in whatever luggage at hand. When my mother woke me up, my only thought was that I wouldn't have to pass my today's exam in mathematics. For an adolescent only half-awake, the invasion of Luxembourg by the Germans triggered a first reflex: "So, I don't have to go to school today!" But this reflex was quickly dissipated by the dramatic moments we had to experience. Very soon, the whole family was gathered on the sidewalk. My uncle David still had his nightshirt under his suit, but in his hands he did not carry a valise, only a prayer book. My father was very nervous. He called on us to be quicker and quicker because he did not want to miss the car which came to fetch us. Suddenly he cried: "The money!" He ran upstairs to take out of the wall safe an envelope with money allowing us to survive for several months. As a matter of fact we all believed that our stay in Arlon would be very short. The car arrived. There were four people already in there and the five of us managed to find a place as well. Some were sitting on the knees of others. Neighbors came out to the street wishing us good luck. But there were also neighbors of German origin, who threatened us with their fists and wished us to go to hell.

To avoid this, operation Arlon had just started!

Indeed. In the car everybody was silent. The son-in-law was driving. He was very nervous for the reason I explained earlier. At the Luxembourg-Belgium border, in Steinfort, there was a roadblock of soldiers. The son-in-law exclaimed: "Merde, les Allemands!" *Shit, the Germans!* A young soldier pointed his gun to us while eating a sandwich. Another one shouted: "Back, back, you cannot go further!" At that moment my father kept his composure. You know, he was courageous in real danger and full of anxiety in imagined danger. He said calmly: "Mr. Officer, we only have the intention to have a cup of coffee in the next village." The soldier, after a short hesitation, let us pass, shouting: "Quick, quick!" The car pursued its path, some of us laughing nervously at the way my father fooled a German soldier and then my aunt Clementine suddenly said, addressing herself both at my father and the owner of the furniture store: "Bravo, Gentlemen. Bravo for your strategic thinking, which led us to the present situation."

Obviously we could not even reach Arlon, which was already occupied by the Germans. So we took another direction and soon we realized that the car with nine people on board would break down before long. So the five of us climbed out and we were alone on the road. It was indeed a pitiful sight. Long columns of refugees started to form themselves on the road: cars, bicycles, as well as mostly carriages drawn by horses. We walked and walked and walked. My father was physically exhausted. He was rather ill at that time and so suddenly he said: "Please, you are younger, pursue the road. I shall return and somehow cope with it."

This of course was out of question for all of us; either we shall perish together or we shall survive together. It was an unwritten law of commitment in my family. That's why some called us the five fingers of the hand. Uncle David and I supported my father and from time to time a carriage drawn by horses took us along for only a few kilometers. Finally, in the late afternoon we arrived in the town of Virton. Completely exhausted, we found rooms in a small hotel. We just learned that the Grand Duchess, her family, and the Luxembourg government had succeeded in escaping the Germans, and that they had passed through Virton a few hours earlier. That was the only good news of the day. That night, lying on a mattress on the floor, I realized to what extent this situation was dramatic and dangerous. In the middle of the night the owner of the hotel woke us up and said: "The Germans are approaching!" So, we left in the dark and on foot we pursued our road, soon reaching the border of France.

Erring on the roads of France

What were your plans at that moment?

Totally exhausted, our immediate target was to reach Montmedy and then Charlesville, where we hoped to catch a train to Paris. In Paris, far from the frontline, we would feel ourselves secure, hoping for some respite and even an end of our ordeal. On the road the refugee columns became longer and longer; most of the time we were walking. I shall never forget the hospitality of the French army in Ecouviers, a small fort of the Maginot line, where the soldiers served us a hot meal, the first since we had left Luxembourg.

In Charleville we caught a train full of people and it took us twelve hours instead of three to reach Paris. The train was attacked by the "Stukas," the fighter planes of the German Luftwaffe. When attacked, the train stopped on the tracks. People were jumping out of the train, crouching in ditches along the railway tracks. Two women were pulling their coat or their sweater over their heads, hoping that this would protect them.

Arriving in Paris, one main objective was reached: you were still alive and you felt yourself secure, at least temporarily. The news from the front line was not very good. The French army had tried unsuccessfully to retain and even to drive back the German army, which succeeded in breaking through the French defense line in Sedan on the fourteenth of May. It was the "Blitzkrieg," or in English, the Lightning War.

In Paris, my father succeeded in contacting a cousin who had taken refuge in Marseille. The cousin's advice was to leave Paris as soon as possible and to go to the west, to Brittany. A train took us the following day to Le Pouliguen, a village on the Atlantic coast. The cousin also told us that living there was less expensive than in Paris. He was right. When we arrived in Le Pouliguen, it was the first time that I saw the ocean. I was deeply moved. We found a small flat in a Britannic house called "Ker Suzanne," belonging to two old ladies who still wore the Britannic attire, "la coiffe bretonne."

We had practically no clothes, no sufficient underwear to change ourselves. Our cousin in Marseille sent us a wooden case with clothes dating from the previous century. The fishermen of Le Pouliguen were amazed and amused at the sight of us. My mother wore with elegance a long dark gown of the nineteenth century. After several days we were accepted by the inhabitants of the village. We even succeeded in becoming an exotic feature of the landscape. We regained hope and thought that we could stay there until the end of the war.

After three weeks, however, we had to leave again. The British expeditionary force which had come to France to rein-force the French army, embarked in order to escape annihilation, as all the French lines of defense had broken down. This was the famous operation "Dunkerque" when the British, including many civilians in ships and boats, succeeded in rescuing and bringing home their army from France. The British, once in their homeland, did not just take a rest but they continued the battle until the Nazis were vanquished. Under the leadership of Winston Churchill, this was Britain's finest hour. An hour which lasted four years. Hitler thought that he could find a compromise solution with Britain. That's why he sent his deputy, Rudolf Hess, on a mission to England, which of course failed as Hess was promptly imprisoned after parachuting on British territory. That was Hitler's first big mistake and the second one was that he thought he could bring the British to their knees. He completely misunderstood the spirit of the British nation, which would never bow to a tyrant. Since that moment and throughout my life, I maintain a feeling of great admiration for Britain, whose language and whose culture, whose writers, poets, and scientists had contributed and continue to contribute significantly to the cultural heritage of humanity.

As far as we were concerned, we felt that in France we were secure nowhere. I literally implored my father to undertake the first formalities in order to obtain an entrance visa for the United States. After some hesitation, because he still kept the hope that we could manage to stay in France, he agreed and we went to the American consulate in Nantes in Brittany to fill out the forms called at that time "first papers." Experience showed us that there were many other papers to be filled out and steps to be undertaken until we succeeded in entering the United States. We decided to reach by any means and as soon as possible the south of France near Marseille or the French Spanish border, possible exits out of France before embarking for the U.S.A. After a few weeks of peregrinations on the roads of France we finally arrived in Montpellier in the "département de l'Hérault," where an office of the Luxembourg Red Cross was established. We stayed there until May 1942, when we succeeded in boarding a ship called the *Maréchal Lyautey* in Marseille, direction Casablanca.

Montpellier or "The symphony in black"

Please, not too fast . . . First, your decision to leave Brittany for Montpellier proved to be right again . . .

Actually, it saved our lives. Soon after we had left Brittany in haste, an armistice was signed between Germany and France, splitting France into two parts: the North, including Brittany and of course Paris, was occupied by the Germans, whereas a smaller part in the South, including Montpellier, the so-called "non-occupied zone," was placed under the authority of the French Vichy Regime of Maréchal Pétain.

. . . and second, according to what you mentioned just before, you spent quite some time in Montpellier.

In my memory, I identify Montpellier of that time with the black color and therefore I used to refer to this period of my life as a "symphony in black."

First because the grapes giving birth to the mellow wine of the Hérault, are black. In autumn, after the harvest, the wine growers poured the grapes into huge barrels and crunched them, while dancing barefoot in the barrels. Black also were the eyes of the women, beautiful women with fiery looks. The elderly women wore black clothes, as in many parts of southern Europe, particularly on the Greek Islands. Last but not least, bleak or black was also our future. We were penetrated by uncertainty and anxiety. We didn't know whether we could ever escape, whether we would succeed in reaching the shores of America.

Could you amplify this? After all, you were in the non-occupied zone of France.

You know, the Vichy Regime had no authority at all. It was completely under the orders of the Germans. It was a fiction and Pétain, in my view, was not a tottering old man but rather quite lucid. He felt at ease with the authoritarian regime of the Nazis, because in his personal ideology, he belonged to the nationalistic right in the French political spectrum. His great enemy was communism and, to a certain extent, the Jews, whom he considered quite dangerous for the French nation. He extolled the virtues of the family and the fatherland ("Travail, Famille, Patrie"). In his view, the Jews were cosmopolitans, migrants, merchants. He did not go as far as his prime minister, Laval, who resolutely collab-

orated with the Nazis, ordering the deportation first of the foreign
Jews, then also of the French Jews to the transit camps in France
or rather the extermination camps in Eastern Europe.

So for you and your family, it continued to be a matter of survival.

Yes, survival in the sense of not being deported but also survival
on a day-to-day basis, because food was scarce. I would not go so
far as saying that there was an immediate risk of dying of hunger.
But being deprived of a minimum of calories causes a general
weakness of your condition, in particular of your immune
system. We were feeding ourselves, yes; I say feeding, not eating
like humans but feeding like animals on strange unknown
vegetables like "rutabagas" and "topinambours." At present,
"topinambours" are served in two or three star restaurants as
noble vegetables of the "haute cuisine." We also flatly refused to
eat a sausage made of blood, called in that part of France,
"sanquet." For Jews it was an abomination but for other human
beings it was a "délicatesse." From time to time we received from
a kind cousin of my father who was a refugee in the Dordogne,
an agricultural part of the south of France, a package of carrots.

That was a feast we reserved for Saturdays, the Jewish Shabbat,
for which we also saved the meager weekly ration of meat. I myself
lost quite a bit of weight at that time and according to what my
parents and friends told me, I turned out to be a rather handsome
young man. But it did not last long. In the United States the wholesome food consisted, as far as my tastes were concerned, to a large
extent of pastry with whipped cream and lots of ice cream. This diet
brought me rather quickly back to my normal physical condition.

What about your studies in Montpellier?

They were erratic, sporadic. Of course I did not risk registration
at the French high school. So without any registration, I followed

the courses on French civilization at the University of Montpellier. Furthermore, I was literally wallowing with delight in German and French literature. I swallowed novels in those languages like the "fin gourmet" swallows oysters, which by the way I don't like at all. I also followed courses in English literature and particularly in literary English, given free of charge to the children of refugees by a professor of Oxford who had retired to Montpellier. I am always indebted to this man who introduced me to and familiarized me with the beauty of the English language. Later, when I arrived in New York, people said "Oh, this young man is speaking the King's English." I must say they did not understand me very well and I did not understand them at all. In Montpellier, where we were staying for about a year and a half, we lived–I would not call it an apartment–in two bedrooms, a kitchen, and a tiny living-room. The toilet was downstairs in the backyard. These lodgings were in a small old house in a suburb of Montpellier quite near the slaughter house. Across the street there was a family living in two rooms and in the kitchen they kept a goat. Our landlord was a couple, rather nice people, who had never seen Jews before. They considered us like strange beings from outer space. Our three furnished rooms were formerly occupied by an old aunt who had left Montpellier. One day the landlord told us that their aunt would return and that we had to leave. This was dramatic for us. We did not immediately find a furnished apartment cheap enough in view of our limited financial resources.

Finally we moved to another place quite distant from where we had been staying. The place was even worse. Just one detail but an important one: the facilities were in the kitchen and the kitchen was a small closet separated by a thin wooden wall from one of the two bedrooms. After a few days–we were in a very dismal, if not a desperate condition–we heard a strange noise on our doorstep. Our former landlord had a dog, a cocker spaniel, which became very attached to us, spending more time with us than with his owners. A whining, peeping sound reached our ears. It was Ketty, the cocker spaniel, who had detected us, who had followed us and found us. We brought him back to the owner, who took us back because apparently the dog would have died if we had stayed away. I still don't know where they put up the old aunt, but all this worked out for us very well and we stayed there until we left for Marseille, the first stopover on our journey to the U.S.A.

Marseille: a Scottish shower and men with a big heart

Thinking back to our stay in Marseille, the so-called Scottish shower comes to my mind. At least in my part of the world, the Scottish shower is known as changing from hot to cold and then again to hot and then again to cold and so on. In our case, "hot" meant: now the U.S. consulate has a visa ready for us. "Cold": there is another complication, another problem to be solved. Indeed, from the time we registered for the first papers at the U.S. consulate in Nantes at the end of May 1940 and after having accomplished all the required formalities, in particular after having obtained from our family in the United States the financial guarantee for the five of us, we still hadn't got the visa in early 1942. You must realize the context: we were in the non-occupied zone and there still was, at least until Pearl Harbor at the end of 1941, a U.S. diplomatic representation in Vichy. If my recollections are correct, Admiral Leahy was the U.S. Ambassador to the Vichy government. But of course after the United States entered the war following the attack in Pearl Harbor, the U.S. Ambassador had been recalled to Washington, but current affairs like the issuance of immigration visas were still accomplished in Marseille, where there was a U.S. consulate.

The U.S. consulate represented the gate to heaven for us, heaven in both definitions of safe harbor but also of paradise. My father and I went, I don't know how many times, from Montpellier to Marseille, waiting in long lines of refugees in front of the U.S. consulate. The queues extended to the sidewalk. The U.S. consulate at that time was located–and this is really quite an astonishing symbol–in a street called "Rue du Paradis," *Paradise Street*. These lines, composed of potential immigrants to the United States, proved to be an easy prey for the French police under the Vichy regime, which could pick out and arrest a number of Jewish immigrants deporting them to French concentration camps, which were the transit for the extermination camps in Germany and Poland.

Of course, the German occupiers were extremely pleased by the way the police under the orders of Vichy performed their tasks. I remember there was a French policeman in civilian clothes who approached my father and asked for his passport. My father didn't show it. The name of Israel, which is our name, would have been a marvelous occasion to arrest us, both my father and myself. So he said that we lost our passport and that we were Luxembourg refugees living temporarily in the south of France before we could return to our country. He also added that in his family, France was always considered as the symbol of freedom and democracy. He explained it to the French policeman in a manner and with a voice, which was really reminiscent of the best theater actors, such as Michel Simon. He added also that his mother–and this was a real fact–died prematurely from a heart attack during the First World War, because she was afraid at one time that France would lose the war. There were tears in his eyes and the eyes of the French policeman were also humid. Result: once more we escaped the worst.

The waiting period for the delivery of the U.S. immigration visa became longer and longer. A new, rather complicated "quota system" was instituted, based on the birthplace and not on the nationality of the potential immigrant, and as a consequence my father, his sister, and me were on the Luxembourg quota list, while my mother and her brother were on the German or Polish list, because they were born in a village which was German before the First World War and Polish after that war. We wrote to the former chief rabbi of Luxembourg, Dr. Serebrenick, who was quite an outstanding man full of dynamism, courage, and dedication to help others. He gave proof of his indomitable courage by personally confronting the infamous Adolf Eichmann, whom he visited in Berlin in order to get an exit visa for members of the Jewish community, who had stayed with him in Luxembourg. That was, I believe, in the year 1941. Eichmann, who was the bookkeeper of the Holocaust, was largely responsible for the murder of millions of Jews. He shouted at Dr. Serebrenick, while sitting in a luxurious office in Berlin: "Jude, stehen bleiben!" *Jew, stop at the door!* Rabbi Serebrenick did not stop but walked down and Eichmann was flabbergasted. He never saw a Jew like that or he never thought that Jews could be like that. Finally Rabbi Serebrenick succeeded in receiving the authorization and hundreds of Jews, thanks to him, were rescued because they could leave Luxembourg under Nazi occupation.

Serebrenick was already established in New York when our letters reached him. He traveled to Washington and at the Immigration department he asked the officer, which one of the two quotas was still open, the German or the Polish? The officer answered the German and then Serebrenick took out of his pocket a document, which was signed under oath, evidencing that Feuerstein, the village where my mother and uncle were born, was German. By the way, if the answer would have been Polish, Rabbi Serebrenick would have pulled out of his pocket another document confirming that Feuerstein was, at the date of the birth of my mother and uncle, Polish and not German.

One can say that a remarkable person like Serebrenick saved your life, since in France your chance of survival would have been very weak.

Absolutely, particularly since the occupation of the so-called free zone by the German army in late 1942. Some Jews survived in occupied France because they were hidden by friendly and very courageous Frenchmen. But the risk was great. If we had stayed, we would probably have perished.

Let me give you another example of what I call the Scottish shower in Marseille. In early May 1942, after almost two long years of anguish and waiting, the immigration visas were delivered to the five of us. Not like today, a stamp on the passport, but a beautiful document on parchment with a red ribbon and the U.S. seal with the American eagle. I can hardly describe the relief and joy we felt, when each of us had this document firmly in his hand, giving us a free passage to the land of the free and the brave.

So we left Montpellier to Marseille several days before May 10, 1942, the day on which we should embark on the French ship, the *Maréchal Lyautey*, for Casablanca. We were staying in a drab cheap hotel in a small side street, very uncomfortable but that was quite unimportant. We counted the hours until the tenth of May 1942.

There was just one more formality to be fulfilled to complete our passport: an exit visa out of France. Normally this would pose no problem once the immigration visa to the U.S.A. was obtained. And then we received a cold, I would say an icy shower. My father, who took our passports to the French relevant authority, had a big smile when entering the office of the competent authority and a few minutes later he came out, his face ashen, crestfallen. Indeed, according to a new order by the German occupier, male nationals of allied nations aged between eighteen and fifty, could not leave France anymore. This concerned me: born on the fifth of May 1924, I had just reached the age of eighteen. Of course, there was no question of separating us or making an amputation of one finger from the hand of the five fingers, as Rabbi Serebrenick called us. But in really dangerous situations my father always showed calm and great resolve. He immediately called his friend, René Blum, a former Luxembourg Minister of Justice who was on the black list of the Nazis and in exile with us in the south of France. René Blum immediately got in touch with the official representative of Luxembourg to the Vichy regime. I think his name was Mr. Funck. The latter went without the slightest delay to see the Interior Minister of the Vichy regime. Both devised a solution. They said that Luxembourg, indeed, had been incorporated into the German Reich. Therefore the prohibition to leave France did not apply to Luxembourgers. One day, before the departure of the ship in Marseille, the five of us received the exit visas; the icy shower became warm again.

The unknown heroes of Gibraltar

You eventually embarked in Marseille on May 10, 1942. Exactly two years after the invasion of Luxembourg by the Germans and the beginning of your peregrination.

That's correct, but on that particular day, we unexpectedly had another cold shower. A German military commission came on board and scrutinized the list of all passengers. Some of them were compelled to leave the ship. Fortunately we could stay and finally we left the harbor and reached the open sea.

Our ship, the *Maréchal Lyautey*, was escorted by two destroyers. We soon reached the Straits of Gibraltar, occupied by the British Army. Suddenly, quite a number of young men, French sailors on our ship, jumped into the sea swimming to the shores of Gibraltar. The two destroyers were pointing their cannons to these courageous soldiers, who went on swimming, ignoring what probably was just a symbolic threat. These sturdy and gallant young Frenchmen who joined the Resistance movement or the Free French forces of General de Gaulle, were representative of the real France, the France fighting for liberty and human rights. But perhaps they remained unknown, perhaps they perished in battles or got well-deserved decorations after the Liberation. Whatever, they remained in my memory as what I would call the unknown heroes. They chose a life of danger rather than the comfort to stay at home under the domination of the Nazis. These young men and I had in common that we were of the same age and confronted with the same enemy. And that's where the comparison stops. They were voluntarily fighting the Nazis while I was a pre-designed victim of our common foe. If this had not been the case, would I have been a volunteer in the Resistance movement? I don't know. But fundamentally, it is a question of the context which determines the position one takes later.

Basically, contexts determine events in history. But contexts change, they evolve, and that is why comparisons with the past are basically wrong, because history is a dynamic and constantly changing process.

From Casablanca to the shores of liberty

Let us come back to earth, or rather to the sea. After having crossed the Straits of Gibraltar, I suppose that the shores of Casablanca were soon appearing on the horizon.

It depends what you understand by soon. It took us two or three days and then we arrived in Casablanca. Getting ashore at that time meant for non-French Jewish refugees passing through a number of controls until we had free passage to the buses wait- ing outside the harbor, not to take us to Casablanca but to one of its suburbs, Ain Sebah, situated on the fringes of what appeared to me to be the desert. During our three weeks stay in Ain Sebah, we only got once a permit to go to Casablanca, a town of which I only have a dim recollection but which I really discovered through the Hollywood classic *Casablanca*, with its unforgettable cast of actors: Humphrey Bogart, Ingrid Bergman, Paul Henreid, Peter Lorre, Claude Raines, Walter Slezak, and many other gifted actors. I have seen that movie picture ten if not twenty times in the United States and later in Luxembourg.

Our three week stay in Ain Sebah was not at all romantic. We all were lodged–about three hundred refugees, men, women, and children–in a large drab room and slept on straw mattresses.

As mentioned before, I had become eighteen years old just five days before our departure from Marseille. In Ain Sebah I smoked my first cigarettes and I also shaved for the first time; not a beard, only some fluffy hair.

This operation took place in the courtyard of our refugee camp, where there was a huge basin with running water, more precisely tepid water, which definitely could not qualify as drinking water. The hygienic conditions there were–and this is an understatement–rather poor. If my recollections are correct, the whole camp had just two toilets, one for men, and one for women.

My father, like quite a number of elderly people, caught some kind of tropic fever there. Fortunately there was a very kind and competent medical doctor among the refugees who treated the sick people. To my father and to those who caught the same illness, he administered quinine. At that time there were neither antibiotics nor penicillin. My father's fever did not go down and we all were deadly afraid that he would not be allowed to board the ship. The day we embarked in the harbor of Casablanca on the *Serpa Pinto*, a Portuguese ship destined for New York, we covered my father with blankets, because he was shivering. But descending from the bus, he took the blankets off his shoulders and walked upright in firm steps aboard the ship. Once we arrived on the lower deck, he nearly fainted in my arms.

Our ship was crammed with passengers. Many slept on deck like myself. My father couldn't and he was put up in a large room practically without any air, where the luggage was normally stored. Yet he survived like many others. How, I don't know. It was some kind of a miracle.

We crossed the ocean in three weeks. In normal circumstances, it would have taken eight days. We stopped at the Canary Islands and later in Hamilton, Bermuda, where a strict passenger control was undertaken in order to detect possible German spies. Both British and American secret service police interrogated every passenger. For me that was quite a fascinating experience and it awoke in my mind stories of spies and criminals.

The ocean was literally infested with German submarines, threatening to sink our ship, if the captain did not agree to put the Jewish passengers in life boats, which would have been easy for the Nazis to sink. Of course, the captain refused. He was a proud Portuguese. But this trip to New York was the next to last the *Serpa Pinto* undertook until the end of the war.

We all knew that we were confronting grave dangers daily, but we did not mind. We had escaped the hell of occupied Europe and the threat to be deported to death camps in Germany or Eastern Europe. Aboard the ship nothing special happened. There was not even a storm. The monotony was broken either through games like tennis or chess or through gossip, which dealt with the usual topic: adultery. Those who indulged in this kind of exercise appeared to me gloating in glee. They were usually elderly and physically unattractive women and men. I reflected on the sources and motives of gossip and came to the conclusion that the fundamental causes of gossip were usually found in some sort of a frustration by those who start it. The same is true as far as the spreading of rumors is concerned.

The monotony was also broken by a happy event. It was the birth of a child, a girl, aboard the ship. This girl, whose parents were Luxembourgers, was called "Serpa" in honor of the name of the ship which took us to the safe heaven of the United States.

The nearer we came to our destination, the more the risks of being sunk by Nazi submarines diminished. What was our feeling as we approached the shores of America? It was a feeling of joy, of gratitude, of fulfillment, and a silent prayer. Finally, first in a dim haze and then clearer and clearer the famous New York skyline appeared. In a split second, in a flash crossing our mind, we realized the deep meaning of America. It is the greatest of all values: "Freedom! Freedom!" Like all the refugees who preceded us and those who will follow us, we all understood that this was the nation where the future of mankind is shaped.

3. Factory Worker

Blue-collar worker

After the understandably deep emotion you felt upon your arrival in the United States, the realities of the day-to-day life–in particular finding a job and generating the necessary resources in order to make a living–imposed themselves. How did you and your family cope with this in a country with a lot of question marks for you?

Before giving an answer to this question, let me just tell you that not so long ago, an American born, bred, and sired in that country and who, like many Americans, is fascinated by Europe and particularly by France, said to me: "You know Edmond, you are idealizing America. You see it through the rosy glasses of the young man who in the forties lived in New York. Your judgment is based on the remarkable record of a great president, Franklin Delano Roosevelt, who not only made an alliance with Winston Churchill and then with Stalin in order to vanquish Hitler, but who, in the early thirties, put into place in the United States a new social system, the New Deal, which to a large extent not only brought relief to those who were in a desperate situation, who were hungry and ill, but which also introduced a number of economic reforms pulling the United States out one of the deepest economic depressions ever experienced by that young nation." My friend went on to say: "Today it is different. There is a lot of poverty and social injustice; a lot of expenses are made in order to wage wars, which are unnecessary. Taxes are cut to benefit a minority of very wealthy people instead of being raised and applied primarily to this privileged segment of the population. So the America of the twenty-first century should not be compared to the America which you experienced during the last World War."

I most definitely do not agree with this judgment because in this reasoning, a very important factor is missing. This factor, rather, this value shaping the policy and destiny of the United States whatever the Administration in power, is "freedom." Freedom to fight for, freedom to be preserved, freedom to be nurtured, particularly in a world where the planet earth seems to shrink in its spatial dimension because of instant communications.

Well, what you just said gives me food for thought, which I have to digest. But just for the sake of the description of your first experiences in the United States, would you kindly agree to revert to my first question: How did you and your family cope with all the problems of daily existence?

Of course philosophical reflections did not permeate the mind of a young man looking for a job. But I had a feeling of freedom and this feeling proved to be a source of energy driving me to meet the challenges of our daily existence.

We realized very quickly that we could not count on others, but had to count first and foremost on ourselves. I was resolved to shun as soon as possible the help we received from institutions or from individuals and to take our destiny in our own hands. This is the American way. It is easier to be said than to be done, and in particular for Europeans completely unprepared for a new type of society.

Right after our arrival we found lodgings and food free of charge thanks to a Jewish institution called "Hias," which was located in downtown Manhattan. The location was certainly not West End Avenue or Westchester County, the residential areas reserved to the wealthy. But we had a roof over our head, a bed to sleep in and food to still our hunger. We shared our sleeping quarters with other refugees where, of course, men and women were separated. For breakfast, lunch, and dinner, we stood in line. I must confess that the food was quite wholesome, and compared to what we had to eat during the war in France, it was of excellent quality even if not "haute cuisine." Perhaps it was too substantial, increasing the cholesterol rate above the normal level. But who at that time cared about this?

What bothered me and also my parents, uncle, and aunt, was the fact that we depended on others. Therefore I quickly looked for a job. I made several attempts. The first was in a factory where, I think, they recycled zippers. I started at 8:00 A.M. At 4:00 P.M. the foreman came up and told me: "You are certainly not mechanically inclined, we can't keep you. So you can pass at the cashier and we shall pay you five dollars for the day." My parents, uncle, and aunt were waiting downstairs. I didn't want to discourage them and when they anxiously asked me how I managed, I said: "Well, I don't like this factory, and therefore I quit."

A second attempt was at a soap powder factory in Hoboken, New Jersey. Here I must open a small paragraph. While in France I was studying at a Jewish training school called ORT. This school started in Russia following the pogroms against the Jews at the beginning of the twentieth century. ORT fanned out in many countries and in some of them this school is still active, particularly in Israel. Anyhow, I studied courses in chemistry and in soap manufacturing there. I still have in my attic the chemical composition of the soap of Marseille.

I presented myself to the company that was hiring. I told them about my studies of soap manufacturing. The man behind the desk nodded his head, and told me that he could make a try with me, starting the following day. When I arrived I thought that they would bring me to a laboratory. Indeed, during the whole preceding night, I had been looking up my notes of soap manufacturing. The next morning at the factory, I was directed to a large hall where workers were filling bags with white soap powder. I was given several of these bags. I had to take the powder with a shovel out of a large container and put it in the bags. I remember that in the evening my nose was irritated and my eyes were red. But the next day and the following days I went on. After a few weeks, I couldn't stand it anymore physically and I quit. I believe that since then I suffer from irritation, sinus trouble, which developed into some kind of chronic allergy.

A week later, I started in another factory. It was located in downtown Manhattan. I had to polish special bullets for machine guns. This was done manually by putting some oily paste on the nozzles of the bullets and then polishing them on special machines. Of course the paste splashed into my eyes. I put on protection. The other workers called our activity "wobbling." So I became a Wobbler. Our work did not require special skills or physical effort. The wages were low, at a strict minimum. Still, I would have stayed on, but two weeks after I was hired the factory went broke.

Thanks to the good advice and intervention of a close friend, I got another job at a small factory, a machine shop, located in Newark, New Jersey. I was completely unqualified for this type of work, but I escaped being fired on the spot because there was a need for manpower. I suffered quite a number of minor injuries in the course of my work, which fortunately did not cause me serious harm. There was, however, one accident where a burning steel splinter entered my eyes and, thanks to God and to an excellent ophthalmologist, I kept my eyesight and was able to resume my work several days after this accident. Each day, one of the owners of the factory walked through the aisles where the machines were installed. He looked over the shoulder of the workers and when he was nearing me I became very nervous, I trembled, and of course was even clumsier than usually. The negative remarks he made in a grumbling voice on my performance sunk directly into my sub-consciousness, because instinctively I did not want to become aware of them. Anyhow, I resisted staunchly all the physical and mental pains I had to endure and went on working in that factory, sometimes sixty hours a week until October 1945, when we had the opportunity to return home to Luxembourg.

Let me add a few memories concerning my contacts with my friend, to whom I owed a job which lasted for more than three years. When we arrived in New York, he was the only one who, the day after our arrival, looked us up at our temporary quarters at the Hias on Lafayette Street. I shall never forget that right from the start he offered to give to my father a power of attorney over his bank account in case we needed some money. Of course my father did not make use of this facility, but it was a very rare gesture of generosity. My friend had two jobs, one in the factory to which he recommended me and a second one as a busboy in a cafeteria. Soon he was drafted into the army and after the war he stayed in it, making a career in the contingent stationed in Germany. He now holds the rank of General.

America: a chosen land, a land unknown

Well, you expanded and elaborated quite a bit on America, its fundamental principles as well as your experiences as a factory worker. I think it would be interesting if you could evoke as well your social life in the United States, your contacts with Americans, in particular with your relatives and friends. After all, the existence of man does not consist only of work.

Indeed, let me illustrate this out of my recollections by a few pictures or flashbacks.

First, our experience with regard to the apartments we rented. The first one we found thanks to an ad in a newspaper. We contacted a man by phone–God bless his soul, he was a good man with a heart, wide and generous. Let me call him Mr. C. He said: "Well, have a look at the apartment." We did not know Manhattan and most definitely ignored that in the early forties West End Avenue was one of the more elegant, residential sectors of New York. We went there and of course the apartment was beyond our expectations. We asked for the rent and he said: "How much can you pay?" We indicated a rather modest but realistic amount, realistic with regard to our means. Then he looked at us with humid eyes and said: "Poor refugees from Europe. I will let this apartment to you for that price." We were elated and the next day we moved in with our few belongings. I must say, we were very happy there and the thought of returning there in the evening compensated for the many deceptions and aggravations I suffered while looking for a job.

After three or four weeks we received a letter from a lawyer by registered mail. It was couched in the legalistic language, yet not menacing or aggressive. It stated that Mr. C. was not entitled to let this apartment to us, because he was only the janitor and his job consisted in relaying the phone calls of those who were interested to rent the apartment to the law office which represented the owner. It went on, mentioning that we could stay if we paid an amount consistent with the space, the furniture, and the location of the apartment. The amount proved to be about five times the one on which the janitor had arranged with us. My father went to see the lawyer, but of course he was not successful. The lawyer said that he would waive any legal proceedings if we left the apartment within a week.

Very much upset, we told this story to the janitor, who said: "Yes, that's the way life is here in America. You are constantly confronted with challenges and to be successful, you need also a bit of luck. Now the luck is that I have another apartment to show to you in a beautiful section of Manhattan, even higher up. It's on Broadway, 125th Street." He had a car and drove us to the apartment. Of course it was not comparable to the one on West End Avenue, but the price was in the range of our financial means. In the description of this flat, Mr. C. was dithyrambic. He said: "It's a jewel. You are in the heart of Manhattan. Could you imagine Broadway, 125th Street? That is higher up Manhattan than the former one on the 60th Street!" He forgot to tell us that the standing of the residential sector of Manhattan did not depend on the level or street number where they were located. Thus 125th Street and Broadway had a much lower status than, for instance, 60th Street. But what could we do? In the evening we packed our clothes into our few pieces of luggage and moved to this new apartment.

Very soon we noted a rumbling noise about every five minutes. We looked out of the window and saw that across the street there was a bridge; the subway train drove from the underground to an elevated bridge and then alongside a few blocks including the one where our apartment building was located. To cut a long story short, in view of our situation we somehow adjusted to the noise. We had no other choice.

About a month later, after we returned from our Sunday afternoon walk in the Bronx Zoo, we found our apartment in a dreadful state. Somebody had broken into our flat. Our clothes were ripped and were lying on the floor. The burglars, obviously mad because they did not find any valuables, gave vent to their anger and deception by tearing apart the few clothes we had. We immediately called the police. A cop, tall, with blue steely eyes, came after two hours. He looked at the havoc and then with a blank stare said to us: "These were not burglars. Probably a bunch of kids or youngsters, who wanted to show you that you are not tolerated in this section of the town. This section is mainly inhabited by Irish. Why don't you move to the Jewish section? That's the advice I give you," and then he departed, a shining Colt dangling on his hips.

We were puzzled, desperate, I would even say, aghast. The next day we went to the "Hias" institution to gather information. We finally learned a lesson: the separation between the various ethnic groups composing the population of New York is deemed to be necessary. The cultural walls dating back to the past have maintained themselves throughout the generations, but beyond these invisible walls all ethnic communities are solidly bound together by their solidarity as American citizens. So, if in different parts of Manhattan they cultivate their traditions and languages of origin, in the end they share common values.

A suitable apartment was shown to us and we rented it. Its location was on West 106th Street between Columbus and Amsterdam Avenue. This was very convenient to us, as our apartment was walking distance from the synagogue called Ramath Orah, which was founded around 1941 by refugees mainly from Luxembourg. Its chief rabbi was Dr. Robert Serebrenick, whom I mentioned before.

A few minutes ago you appeared to me to be idealizing America a little bit. Does the day-to-day reality as described by you through your own experiences not deny this idealistic description?

Not at all. Like a portrait of Rembrandt, life is made of light and shadow, but in America light prevails. It is freedom for everyone.

It should be stressed that during the period I spent in the United States, this country was at war. America was engaged on two fronts, in the Pacific and in Europe. At home, men aged from eighteen years on were drafted in the army. Military service was compulsory. Also refugees who did not have American nationality were drafted. I appeared several times before the draft board, but got a deferment because I had to support my family.

In the U.S. homeland families were worried and many were in grief, because they lost their loved ones.

In the present time there is a tendency to forget the sacrifices the United States made for the preservation of democracy and freedom worldwide. We should not forget that so many cemeteries in Europe and in the Pacific region are covered with white crosses and stars of David. Unfortunately Alzheimer's disease does not only affect individuals. There is also a kind of political Alzheimer's disease which affects nations and political leaders.

A feeling of solidarity bound all Americans, whatever their ethnic background, their color, or their creed. There were numerous girls who became pen pals of the soldiers abroad. Entertainers such as Bob Hope and Bing Crosby and many others brought the smell and taste of home, a warming sense of humor, to those who were risking their lives day and night in foxholes, on battlefields, on ships, and planes for the preservation of freedom and for the liberation of those who were oppressed, like my countrymen in Luxembourg. For instance, there were scenes of wild joy, of overwhelming enthusiasm in the streets of Paris and all the towns and villages when they were liberated by the U.S. army. But this enthusiasm unfortunately was dampened very quickly through politics.

In the United States we closely followed the development on the battlefields. At that time a feeling of deep friendship grew between the peoples of the United States and of the Soviet Union. Women's organizations under the guidance and leadership of the wife of the President Roosevelt, Eleanor, were knitting woollies for the Soviet soldiers, who confronted the German armies in the coldest of all winters. We all followed on the radio with anxiety and hope the outcome on the battlefields in the Soviet Union. Soviet military leaders like Marshall Zhukov or General Timochenko were heroes for us. Here again, after Yalta things changed, politics took over, and what might have been an opportunity to create a real enduring peace between East and

West was soon shattered by so-called national interests. The Cold War between East and West broke out and lasted for nearly half a century.

After Stalingrad, the winds most definitely turned in favor of the Allies. At that time the Luxembourg government in exile opened an embassy in Moscow. The first Ambassador was our friend René Blum, Minister of Justice before the war in Luxembourg. He looked up my father and also spoke to me asking us whether I could come with him as his personal assistant to Moscow. The condition of course was that I had to learn the Russian language in a very short period of time. He presented me a textbook and I registered in evening courses at a specialized school in New York. This was a dream; it lasted several weeks, and then I gave up. I was too tired to follow intensive evening courses after my work at the factory. But the real reason was that I didn't want to leave for Moscow and to abandon my family, in particular my sick father, in New York.

Let me further give you a flashback on the contacts with our relatives and some friends of the Jewish community. To our relatives we owe an eternal debt of gratitude for allowing us to come to the United States. They saved our lives, they saved us from being deported and probably gassed by the Nazis, which is certainly worse than being killed by a bullet.

We saw our relatives from time to time. They were very nice to us, but they had their own life and that's what we did not understand right away. We thought that they had to be more at our disposal. We adjusted gradually, sometimes a bit painfully to our new life.

Sidney, a cousin of my father who had granted the five of us the financial guarantee, had a niece who lived with her mother and grandmother on Lincoln Avenue in Brooklyn. They invited us from time to time on Friday evenings for the "Shabbat dinner." Hortense was a bright young woman who worked as secretary for her uncle Sydney. She was a pen pal of a young soldier who fought the war in the Pacific and whom she married after the war. At these dinners, my father, who along with quite an array of other illnesses, was also a diabetic, had to eat a special bread called gluten bread. That's why Hortense and her mother called him "Gluten Gustav." They were warm-hearted and naive, and the nickname they gave to my father was a special brand of a sense of humor which took us quite a bit of time to digest.

Did you have a girl friend in those days? I can hardly imagine that you spent your time only between the factory and the family.

I must say that most of my leisure time, I spent with my family. Sometimes I went out alone, encouraged by my mother. I met and sometimes dated girls at the Jewish community of Ramath Orah. However, I felt particularly attracted by two girls who worked with me at the factory. One was of Polish origin and the other one had Greek parents. The latter was beautiful and sexy. One day at the Christmas party offered by the factory owner to the workers, things became wild and dangerous between several factions of workers, all fighting for the favors of these two girls. Knives were pulled out of pockets. I ran away and since then my relationship with these two attractive girls was essentially platonic.

I was and still am a dreamer. Behind my lathe, I was dreaming of our return to Luxembourg, of a quiet and studious life as a white-collar worker, preferably as a well-protected employee in the governmental or municipal administration.

But the main part of my dreams was devoted to philosophy. I was intellectually groping my way through the hazy maze of philosophical theories that my father, even in his state of physical illness, continued patiently and passionately to explain to me. Working my way through all this and trying to shape my own philosophy was an ongoing process which lasts until today.

"Next year in Luxembourg"

If I had to ask you to summarize in a few words your experiences, I mean your life in the United States, what would you say?

I would say two words: "gratitude" and "hope." Gratitude towards a nation, which is based on the fundamental principle of freedom. Freedom of choice being the main, if not the essential source of energy, allowing everyone to go on living and to meet the many challenges for a successful life. And for us, Luxembourg refugees, the hope, thanks to America, to return to our country. A prayer the Jews recited several times on Passover is: "The next year, in Jerusalem." We, in America, were praying: "The next year, in Luxembourg."

Speaking about Luxembourg, do you recall among your encounters in the Luxembourg section of the congregation in New York some instances which left a specific imprint in your memory?

Yes. They are linked to the visits paid to us and the gatherings made for us by members of the Luxembourg government in exile or other exiled Luxembourg officials. Their presence cemented the links binding us to our country. From time to time we had a party where the Luxembourg national dish, the "gekachte Kéis," *cooked cheese,* was the main, if not the only course of the dinner. The cooked cheese was salted by so many tears which poured out of our eyes. We also cried with emotion and pride when the New York newspapers, one morning in 1942, head-lined on the front pages: "First general strike by the smallest allied nation, Luxembourg."

But it was only in 1945 that we were able to return to our homeland. To be precise, in October 1945, on a Norwegian Cargo ship called *Ida Backe*, where the stewards let us have their cabins, a testimony of solidarity to refugees returning to their homeland. After crossing the ocean, this time not infested by Nazi submarines, we arrived in Antwerp, which was to a large extent destroyed by the V-1 and V-2 rockets, which Hitler asked his specialist, Wernher von Braun, to develop as the ultimate weapon. After the war the American Space Agency hired Wernher von Braun, who devised rockets for interplanetary missions. In Antwerp a train took us first to Brussels, where we did not stay for more than one day, and then to Luxembourg.

What were your feelings on that train, particularly when approaching Luxembourg?

Mainly a mixed feeling made of bliss and uncertainty. It was similar to the one we had on the *Serpa Pinto* when we were nearing the shores of America. But the source of our feelings this time was different. Approaching America, it meant for us freedom and a land unknown. Approaching Luxembourg, the source of our feeling was happiness to be back home after five long and eventful years, as well as uncertainty about how we would be received by our compatriots. In what condition would we find our house and all that rightfully belonged to us, and how would we organize our life to make a new start?

Leaving the train, we were not crying, because our emotions were pent up, locked in our mind and soul, unable to find an outlet by tears. We were struck by the fact that Luxembourg City did not look much different from the one we left. A taxi took us to our house, which was occupied by a former tenant and by some families, which the Luxembourg authorities had temporarily installed there. The attics were unoccupied, so that we could establish ourselves there, in the house which we owned. And this persisted for several weeks until the temporary tenants had found other lodgings. In the neighborhood people showed us a lot of sympathy. Was this sincere or not? It was difficult to say. The cellar of our house was full of dust and dirt, but the worst of the dirt was the Nazi propaganda literature which the Germans could not dust away as they had to leave Luxembourg City hastily at the liberation by the U.S. army. During the war, our house was confiscated by the Nazi occupiers and one of the sections of VDB, the "Volksdeutsche Bewegung," was installed there.

Walking in the streets of Luxembourg City, more specifically walking in the suburbs, I met often long columns of people who looked depressed and who did cleaning work. They were obviously prisoners and were pointed out to us as collaborators. Some people self-righteously pounded their breast and said in a loud and resounding voice: "These are Nazis, traitors. If I had to make the decision, I would have shot them." Later we were told that those who were the most outspoken in their aggressiveness were perhaps themselves not so irreproachable. They turned out to be staunch supporters of the Allies after the battle of Stalingrad and when the first tanks of General Patton were nearing Luxembourg. I myself could not develop any feeling of hatred against those branded as great criminals to the public eye. As a matter of fact, I felt neither hatred nor pity. I don't know what I felt, but I believe that some of them should have been brought to court, not just herded like sheep and compelled to do forced labor without any trial. But it is unjust of me to pass a judgment on this, because during the Nazi occupation in Luxembourg, I was in France, then safely in the United States until the end of the war.

Another picture, very vivid in my memory, is the empty square, where the Synagogue of Luxembourg stood before it was destroyed by the Nazis. Until its reconstruction on another spot, a religious Jewish service was first held at a place which became the "Théâtre des Capucins" and then on the ground floor of a one-story building which later became the Trading Floor of the Luxembourg Stock Exchange, until it was torn down to make a place for a supermarket.

Weren't you shocked at the thought that a place of prayer became a trading floor of the Stock Exchange and then a supermarket?

For me any place can be a place of prayer and meditation; a sanctuary is a place where people are not killed, a place of peace and justice. That's a very important thought for me, in particular in our time, in the twenty-first century, when people commit crimes for the sake of keeping sanctuaries untouched. God, the ultimate Reality, is everywhere and not bound to any specific place or building.

Coming back to your personal life, what were your first efforts to reinsert yourself into the society?

I first tried to resume my studies after an absence of nearly four years. I had to prepare myself to pass the "baccalauréat," the final high school examination. I had several months at my disposal, and then I passed it thanks to a program which was created for those who had to leave their country because of their religion or those who were drafted into the Nazi army. I passed it successfully, in particular because my teachers gave me good marks on my essays written in French and in English relating our experiences in France and in the United States. They were very tolerant regarding mathematics, chemistry, and physics. Anyhow, I got the "baccalauréat," which opened to me the doors of the universities in neighboring countries.

But as we know, you did you not pursue your studies. Can you explain why?

First of all, I did not want to leave my family. After the war the links which united us were stronger than ever before. But that was not the main reason. In all honesty, I really did not want to go to the university. Was it out of laziness, was it because I was afraid? Who really knows after so many years? The fact is that I am an autodidact. Not by accident, but by nature. And so, I looked for a job.

And your family, your father and uncle?

My uncle resumed his activities as a traveling salesman in textiles. My father, who was diminished, not intellectually but physically, could not resume his professional activities. He gave counsel and advice, and helped, thanks to his numerous contacts in the government, not only our family but a number of refugees who survived the war.

He passed away in 1949. In the evening before his death he asked me for the book written by the German philosopher Leibniz and read, though he had strong physical suffering, the part of the theory of Leibniz on the "Monads." He was fascinated all his life by this theory in particular and peacefully he passed away. I had the distinct feeling, even conviction, that at last he succeeded in finding the way to reconcile philosophy based on science with faith.

In the evening after his burial my mother recalled to me a story of my childhood.

When I was a little child, my parents, uncle, and aunt liked to go out on Saturday evenings from time to time to a place where they could find some amusement. At that time there was no baby-sitting facility, except for the very wealthy. So, alternatively one of the couples stayed at home with me. One evening, I was perhaps six or seven years old, it was my mother and father's turn to go out. I don't remember how, but I succeeded in escaping the vigilance of my uncle and aunt and running to a dance hall called the "Majestic" where I knew that my mother and father would spend the evening. It was a very popular place, where the Luxembourgers spent an amusing evening dancing to the tunes of tangos and Vienna waltzes. Breathless, I ran up the stairs to the first floor and to my greatest dismay I saw my mother dancing with a man who was not my father, while my father was dancing with a woman who was a stranger. A burning thought flashed through my mind: that was the end of everything. My parents would separate. They would divorce and leave me alone. Yes, I had the egoistic feeling of every child whose parents are about to divorce: "What will happen to me?"

I cried and shouted with a loud and shrill voice. The music stopped. The dancers froze on the spot. Nobody knew what exactly happened. My mother was the first to react. She saw me, ran to me, asked what happened and in a crying and whining voice, I explained to her the reason for my affliction. She started to laugh and explained that my father and she just went out with a couple of friends and each one was dancing with the partner of the other and that was it. Nothing was changed, not in the slightest manner, in the relationship between my father and herself.

After having recalled this incident, my mother said: "You see, Edi, destiny has finally separated us. This could have happened earlier. God was kind to us and so we survived many trials, many dangers and in spite of the poor state of health of your father, we were able to stay together until today. The moments we spend with those who are close to us are counted. They are precious. When God takes, we must accept. On the other hand, when God gives, we must not hesitate to grasp the opportunity, knowing that the countdown has started already."

This thought, on the evening after the burial of my father, left a deep imprint on my way of thinking, on my way of living. And keeping this in mind, I developed a passion of life, which I call in this book: "In love with life."

4. An International Banker in Luxembourg

Fifty years of banking

You told me that when you were a lathe turner in Newark, New Jersey, you were dreaming to become, once back in Luxembourg, a white-collar worker, preferably an employee in a governmental or municipal administration, socially well-protected. As a child and young man you wanted to become a teacher. Finally you became a banker in Luxembourg, a surprising U-turn. How did this happen and how did you cope with it?

I entered the banking profession more by necessity than inclination. When I was looking for a job after the war, my father was making some contacts. First, in a state-controlled social insurance institution where they were looking for young men to pursue a quiet and perhaps, at the end, a financially rewarding career. But I did not succeed in getting the job; I was told that I was overqualified. That was a nice way to put it; probably they meant underqualified. Anyhow, I did not get the job. Then my father took an appointment with one of the leading people of a bank in Luxembourg–by the way, not the bank where I pursued my career. He was told: "Your son deserves to make a successful career. He cannot do that if he does not have a university diploma. Therefore I strongly advise you to have your son pursue studies, and once he has completed them and received a diploma, for instance in economics, come back and hopefully I will then have an opening for him." This advice might not have been so bad, but anyhow neither my father nor I followed this recommendation. So, pursuing his contacts, my father spoke to one of the directors of Banque Internationale à Luxembourg. This man, Joseph Leydenbach, later became president of the bank. He is counted among the builders of Luxembourg's economy and banking in the postwar era. At the same time he was a writer and a poet, as well as a cello player, a man of many talents. He granted me an interview. He was very kind and asked me whether I had any experience in banking. I said no. And then he asked me if I spoke fluent English and I said yes. A few days later, he hired me. And that's how my professional career started.

At that time banking in Luxembourg was purely national, to a certain extent parochial. So were the mentalities, except for a few, like Joseph Leydenbach, who was very international in his outlook, highly cultured, open-minded. Joseph Leydenbach left a lasting imprint on the Banque Internationale à Luxembourg. Through his personal example he showed that an executive in a bank or in another institution does not need to be a specialist in his field. He must be creative, forward looking, intuitive, and this was certainly the case with this outstanding personality.

Could you explain how the banking activity in general and your own activity in particular were performed at that time, in the late forties?

I really do not intend to dwell too long on this part of banking. Perhaps giving a brief overview of my own activities in the late forties and early fifties would be the best illustration how in the "Banque Internationale à Luxembourg" and similar banks business in Luxembourg was conducted. I happened to be in contact with customers very early, not just making current operations, but trying to give them to the best of my knowledge–or rather by intuition–some advice on how they should invest. Why do I say out of intuition? Because at the beginning my knowledge was very fragmentary. At that time, one did not rely so much on charts and on figures.

My first promotion after the first few years was to be allowed go to the teller where we served customers for investment operations, except those who were very important and who had access to a manager in a private office. Among my customers I want to single out one category, retired people, particularly widows. They took a liking to me. And some of these very nice ladies took quite a bit of my time. In the beginning I did not mind; later on it got on my nerves, but I could not show it.

Once I had a rather unusual but also interesting and somewhat disturbing experience. One of the female customers who sometimes were standing in line before my teller told me: "Well, I want to make a special investment and people around here do not need to listen to what I say. Why don't you have a cup of coffee or tea at my home?" I went to her home with my briefcase. Her husband, a tall, good looking man in the early sixties received me with a blank stare in his eyes. He said: "Oh, you are Edmond Israel and you want to see my wife. Just a second, I will call her." And then in the beautiful villa this couple owned, he went upstairs and called his wife who came down. She was flustered: "Well, that's kind of you, Mr. Israel, that you take your spare time for my little problem. Before we get into finance, could you tell me a little bit about yourself? You know, I trust you and I think the advice you gave me the other day was quite good. But I want to know more about the people with whom I deal." "Well," I thought to myself, "be careful." I gave her a brief summary of my life in particular as a refugee in France and in the United States. Then right away I came back to the object of my visit, that is investing in stocks. In the meantime she apologized. It was a summer evening, rather hot. She changed her gown into a rather flimsy one with a generous décolleté.

Dutifully I took out the list of securities, stocks, and bonds I was recommending at that time. She bent over me. She had a rather strong perfume which I did not find pleasant and I coughed. Still today I am allergic to certain types of perfume. She noticed that her approach was not successful, but did not say a word. I knew that I had to be careful. It was a real balancing act on a razor's edge. These people were influential. So finally in a loud voice, so that her husband could hear me on the first floor, I described the bonds–their maturity, their interest rate, their yield–as well as the stocks. At that time I already particularly favored triple-A (AAA) American equities. After having taken another sip of coffee, I looked at my watch and said: "I am terribly sorry, but I have to look up another customer." I just wanted to make her understand that I was not making an exception for her. She had a smile on her face. It was ironic, kind and resigned at the same time. I think she realized that I was too young and probably naïve and inexperienced with women. We remained on good terms and from time to time, she came to the teller and asked my advice, but that was all and I felt relieved.

OK, but now I would like to hear more about the techniques in banking. How was the securities back office handled, for example? At that time there was no computer, nothing automatic.

Indeed, in the Securities department where I had my desk, a man, who had been at the bank much longer than I, was in charge of securities bookkeeping. He was physically strong, which was important because he had to carry huge heavy ledgers where all the transactions were recorded. In a beautiful handwriting, he couched artfully in blue ink the transactions on the white paper of the securities ledgers. Besides calligraphy he also had the gift to be an excellent trumpet player in a suburban band of Luxembourg. He also knew how to tell jokes in a flowery and somewhat poetic language which made us laugh. When the head of department entered the room, the laughing stopped abruptly, and we all bent over the files on our desk.

At that time the female employees were mostly doing secretarial work on typewriters. Professionally they were on the lower end of the hierarchical ladder. They had to wear long, ugly linen shirts at work, mainly in dark grey or black. One of the female employees was an exception, because she succeeded to become the secretary of the General Manager and later of the Chairman of the board. She also had the task to supervise the attire of the female employees. She was a spinster, severe with those under her authority, and quite efficient in the exercise of her duties. We, the male employees, had fantasies from time to time, imagining sexy underwear under the long and drab shirts of the girls.

Perhaps the time has come now where we could talk about the process which led the banks in Luxembourg to develop international activities.

I suggest we come back to this when I shall evoke the origin and the present state of banking and financial activities in Luxembourg. To conclude the part describing my banking career, I would say that as soon as the conditions for international activities arose in Luxembourg, my position at Banque Internationale took a U-turn. I mounted the hierarchical ladder quickly and progressively. In the span of ten to fifteen years, I became department head, manager, general manager, as well as a member of the executive board of our bank. My career and the development of the international financial activities in Luxembourg were very much interwoven. This was by chance and by necessity, because there were not so many colleagues who had a good command of English. I was entrusted with the negotiations regarding the administrative functions of the first Eurobond issue. My direct involvement in this process, which was fascinating, led me to think less of philosophy and to be rather implicated in the construction of a segment of Luxembourg's economy, which over years and decades proved to be sustainable and essential for my country. Indeed Luxembourg now has and I believe will also have in the future, the benefit of international financial activities by far beyond the size of the country. But now I am anticipating my forthcoming developments.

Luxembourg's financial center, a passion to construct

• Origins

You are associated by many in and out of Luxembourg with its financial center. You have been one of the promoters, actors as well as privileged witnesses of this quite astounding occurrence. This was from the early sixties until your partial retirement in the mid-nineties, a fascinating period during which the technological revolution took place as well as a stupendous growth of banking in Luxembourg.

Don't be afraid. I won't cite too many figures, nor shall I enter into many technical details. This is the job of historians and specialists, and I do not count myself in this category. As I am an autodidact, I shall stick to my guns and try to give a more general overview of the origins and various phases which led to the emergence and progressive expansion and growth of international banking in Luxembourg. At the beginning, we were considered by many in and outside of Luxembourg as dreamers, utopians, not to be taken seriously. It was an attitude of benign neglect as well as compassionate indulgence. In the course of time this attitude changed. Why it changed is reflected in my present narrative.

The financial center of Luxembourg has not fallen from heaven like manna in the desert. Luxembourg was far from being a desert as far as the legal and operational infrastructure for international banking activities was concerned. Our ancestors already had the vision of international financial operation in their minds when creating the Luxembourg Stock Exchange in 1929. It could not be viable in a country as small as Luxembourg. So listing of foreign securities and cross-border transactions were already anticipated, but could not became reality until after the last World War and more specifically until the emergence of the Eurobond market in the early sixties.

• Birth

Luxembourg's banking center has a history and a potential. Luxembourg had to find the context in order to realize its potential. This context was the Eurobond market, which emerged in the early sixties, due to the creativity of international bankers, such as Siegmund Warburg in London. They realized that the time had come when transactions and investments would take place across borders, calling for an efficient infrastructure in instant communications. So is it the technological revolution which brought about this market? No. The emergence of the market is essentially due to the creativity of some outstanding bankers. Yet the market could only evolve as technology allowed transactions to be conducted on a large scale transnationally and even transcontinentally.

In Luxembourg we offered several interesting conditions, particularly for the listing on our stock exchange, as well as the safekeeping of securities and a number of other functions in this context. Like many innovations, the Eurobond market met a heavy dose of skepticism. That's what I call old thinking. We Luxembourgers are usually not skeptical. So, we were ready to engage ourselves in a new line of activities–I would not even call it a venture. We are prudent and cautious people. We leave venturous activities to others.

During the postwar era a number of profound changes took place in Luxembourg. We had to rebuild our country, at least partially, and also adapt our economy to the conditions of that time. Mentalities changed progressively, perhaps not at a fast pace, but profoundly. Luxembourg became international. Luxembourg also became European through the implementation in our country of the first European institution, the European Coal and Steel Authority. We were among the six founding member countries. We also benefitted from a stable social climate which, as history tells us, was not the case in some of the neighboring countries. The moment had arrived when the vision of our forefathers to become international in banking and finance could be fulfilled. Let me recall that in 1929, legislation was enacted in Luxembourg permitting the creation and functioning of international holding companies. The holding company proved to be an important instrument for the conduct of certain financial operations. Of course this legislation had to be adapted to a changing environment. It should be stressed that the principle of transparency and the avoidance of the use of holding companies for purposes not consistent with the legal requirements in our country as well in the countries of the promoters were priorities for the changes in the legislation of holding companies.

Furthermore, the Luxembourg Stock Exchange was also founded in 1929, which could fulfill the role imagined by the founders only much later, thanks to the Eurobond market. Here again, as far as our banking center is concerned, the principle–or should I call it a law of nature–"Nothing is permanent but change" applies. The bedrock, an appropriate legal and administrative framework, existed already but had of course to be adapted. That was the Luxembourg environment when the attention of the initiators and promoters of the first phase of international capital market operations, the Eurobond market, was drawn to Luxembourg.

Nineteen-sixty-three proved to be the turning point from domestic to transnational and even transcontinental banking. In a general manner the Eurobond is an instrument of financing and investment not necessarily denominated in the currency of the issuer. It is also placed both with private and institutional investors on a number of transborder market places. In the early sixties, skeptics considered these issues as being somehow homeless. They were considered orphans. Because of the requirements for institutional investors to buy and to hold only securities listed on an official market, the necessity arose to turn to a stock exchange. After many explorations and investigations, the Luxembourg Stock Exchange proved to offer the best conditions, and so the first Eurobond issue, Autostrade, was listed on our Exchange. This marked the start of an evolution leading Luxembourg to become an international banking and financial center recognized and even coveted by other important centers in and outside of Europe. Just two figures: in 1963, about 150 securities were listed on the Luxembourg Stock Exchange. At the end of 2004, the number of listed securities, of which Eurobonds and shares of investment funds constitute the bulk, exceeds the staggering figure of 33,000.

Some call the Eurobond market a saga. If this saga was presented as a movie, the first act could be situated in New York, the second in London and the third simultaneously in Luxembourg as well as on a number of other market places.

Why the first act in New York?

Because after the war, the main issuing activity of bonds denominated in U.S. dollars took place in New York. Foreign borrowers for long term financing turned to New York and the bonds were mainly placed in the U.S.A. But in the wake of recurrent deficits of balance of payments in the United States, a feature which appears to be permanent in that country, the U.S. administration of President John F. Kennedy introduced a tax, the well known "interest equalization tax," which the American investors had to pay on the interest paid out on bonds in U.S. dollars issued by foreign entities. That's the end of the first act.

The second one took place in London. Astute and creative bankers like Siegmund Warburg perceived that this was now the right moment to shift this activity from New York to London and the European continent. Of course, Siegmund Warburg had already thought for quite some time that the dormant short-term placed U.S. dollars originating from the U.S. Marshall Plan were waiting for an opportunity, like the Eurobonds, assuring a higher return. A technological infrastructure for transborder and transcontinental transactions existed in the limbs, but of course was not as sophisticated as we know it nowadays, thanks to the evolutionary process of science and technology, moving everything at a constantly faster pace. Siegmund Warburg and his associates visited a number of potential European borrowers and finally raised an interest in Italy. And that's how the Autostrade issue was realized. Siegmund Warburg, both a dreamer and a realist, was convinced that he could not conclude such an operation alone. The syndicate must also include banks outside of London. Thus the managing syndicate of the $15,000,000 Autostrade bond issue, 5.5%, 1963-1978, was composed of S.G. Warburg/London, Amro Bank/Netherlands, Deutsche Bank/Germany, Bank of Brussels/Belgium, Lazard Frères/France, and Banca Comerciale/Italy. No trumpets were blown at the birth of the Eurobond market and yet, this first Eurobond issue heralded a new era in banking and finance.

The curtain falls again. *Third act.*

After the official listing of the Autostrade bonds on the Luxembourg Stock Exchange, new actors–Luxembourgers–appear on the stage. They were mostly unknown outside of the banking world. Among those actors, I count myself among the least known at that time. I treaded cautiously on unknown ground and was testing uncharted waters, which were particularly dangerous as I don't know how to swim. At the beginning it was only a matter for me of negotiating the procedures to list these bonds on our Exchange. But the whole structure of this issue with a management syndicate, an underwriting, and also a selling group was not well known in our center. As a matter of fact, it took me quite some time to understand all its implications. Some of my superiors asked me: "What does that mean, underwriting group?" I said in French: "Syndicat de Garantie." That raised some eyebrows: "You never told us, Mr. Israel, that our bank must guarantee this issue. You should have done that." I did not panic, but was on the verge of it. Soon I learned that it only meant to guarantee the placement of the bonds, which was anyhow practically assured. I was given a second chance, not only to stay in the bank but also in this field of international activities.

Thinking back to these pioneering times, I must say that I had a double function in the role I assumed both with gusto and anxiety. I had to explain in Luxembourg the structure and the mechanics of financial operations, which I slowly and only progressively started to understand myself. Abroad, and particularly in London, I had to explain Luxembourg, which was easier for me. As main arguments I mentioned not only the multicultural environment as well as a stable social climate, but also the fact that we were experimenting in Luxembourg with some sorts of international instruments, for instance units of account, in which bonds placed on more than one market were denominated and listed on our exchange. In order to increase the chances for the Luxembourg Stock Exchange to be selected for the listing of Eurobonds, I stressed the international expertise and skills already prevalent at that time in Luxembourg. I don't want to overrate my role in this, because I believe that to a certain extent the minds in favor of Luxembourg were already made up. The broker to the issue was Strauss Turnbull. The main partner, Julius Strauss, was, like Siegmund Warburg, a German banker of

Jewish faith. Both left Germany because of the threat from the Nazis and established themselves in London, where they became very successful.

In the third act, the curtain doesn't come down because the play or movie continues until today. Perhaps it could be compared to an unachieved symphony having no end, but many composers from generation to generation.

• **Growth**

You have developed until now one type of operations, Eurobonds. There are many other activities which in the course of time have emerged and represent a substantial part of Luxembourg's financial and banking activities. Could you elaborate on this?

With the greatest pleasure. Shakespeare said "All the world's a stage." I think that banking and finance on our globe is a formidable stage. The actors are numerous. They are reflections of humanity. Some are creative and have the highest regard of good conduct, of ethics. Others crave to make more and more money. In their greed, they do not shrink from activities which do not fit in the mold of a legal and regulatory framework. They are scoundrels. You find them in all wakes of human activity. Over the years on this stage of global banking appeared and continue to appear a number of more and more sophisticated operations and products.

In Luxembourg, the Eurobond sector was progressively joined by international credits as well as investment funds linked to private banking. In all these areas, Luxembourg has proven to be strong and effective in administrative and distributing functions, perhaps less as far as the set up of operations and the creation of new products are concerned. The same applies to the intellectual side, in portfolio management. For a number of years I have said and written that this is a very promising segment where we could compete successfully because we have the experience and also, what I consider even more important, an international outlook and a cautious way in handling other people's money. We are not venture minded and I think that most of the people who entrust to the bank part or even all of their assets to be managed are more conservative than quick profit-minded. Of course I am generalizing here, but I think that if we leave the risky part of that business to others who probably have more experience and know-how in this than we, there is no harm. It's certainly better than to be inactive in this promising sector of intellectual portfolio management.

As far as international credits are concerned, Luxembourg was selected by foreign banks particularly because in Luxembourg the banks did not have the obligation to deposit part of their assets interest-free with a Central Bank. I think there are also quite a number of other reasons which pleaded in this sector for Luxembourg, but I don't want to go into these details, at least not in the context of this book.

Another reason for the fast and even surprising growth of banking in Luxembourg was that it became fashionable for foreign banks to have an operational base in Luxembourg, even for such banks which in their head office had not yet engaged in global banking or international credits. Some of them closed the doors of their branches or subsidiaries in Luxembourg within a rather short span of time. During the period from 1960 to 1996, the number of banks established in Luxembourg rose from 17 to 221 and the number of employees in the banks from 1,300 to over 20,000.

At the time of my writing this English version of my book *La Vie, passionnément*, the number of banks has slightly declined. This phenomenon is due mainly to the mergers of some banking groups having an impact on the branches and subsidiaries in Luxembourg. On the other side, a number of activities have broadened in scope and also many others have appeared. For instance, the so-called structured products have considerably widened the array of investment instruments since the late nineties. This is a most interesting and promising development. So all in all, the activities of the Luxembourg banking and financial center are both on solid ground as well as expanding.

Could you now evoke what your role has been in this impressive sector of the Luxembourg economy and even beyond the borders of Luxembourg?

I am not particularly fond of stressing and highlighting what some consider as a crucial role by myself in the evolution and growth of international banking of Luxembourg. So let me rather describe some of my activities in this field. I do not want to repeat myself, therefore I won't come back to the birth of the Eurobond market, but it really was a motor driving me to go on describing and explaining to many bankers abroad the conditions and facilities Luxembourg offers in this context. I did this through the medium of publications in specialized magazines and reviews, but mainly on the occasion of meetings with other bankers as well as when I was invited to deliver presentations in international conferences. Colloquia and workshops in international banking started to become increasingly frequent during the early sixties. By now we experience an explosion of such events, and I am wondering to what extent attendance will not slacken, unless the topics are new and point to the future.

So through these activities I gradually became the unappointed ambassador for our banking center. The tasks I voluntarily assumed were difficult but also challenging and exciting. In my speeches I tried to focus on some catch-phrases. I remember that in front of a gathering of Asian bankers, I coined the phrase "Banks are people." It was very well received and in the midst of my presentation, there was applause. Sometime later I heard this phrase quite a number of times being pronounced by others. Were they copying me? I don't know. As a matter of fact, I don't believe so. I think ideas crop up spontaneously when the context for such reflections arises.

On the lighter side, let me just mention two events. My trips often took me to London. Ties of friendship developed with quite a number of bankers. One of the builders of the international capital market, a London banker of German origin once invited me and my first wife, Raymonde, for a cup of tea in one of the most exclusive hotels in London. Suddenly, Raymonde, in a frightened voice, said: "A mouse. She just ran over my feet." Our host, not even raising his eyebrows, just said: "Absolutely impossible here." Then his wife who also attended the tea said: "Well, Raymonde is right. I saw the mouse, running to the other side of this room." Our banking friend reacted by saying: "I can't believe it." We finished our tea. Our host looked at his wristwatch: "Really, I am sorry I have to leave now." He called the waiter, paid the bill, and gave him his visiting card while asking him to pass it on to the manager. He would appreciate it if the latter called one of these days.

The cultural background and upbringing in the childhood leaves a deep imprint on all of us. My friend of German origin did not take this rather amusing event lightly. His inborn sense of duty induced him to report it to the management of the hotel. If my friend would have been born, bred, and sired in Her Majesty's country, he would probably have reacted with a flippant remark somehow downplaying the whole event.

Another event took place, I think, in the seventies. There was one of the numerous meetings in Luxembourg of a European Institution, probably in charge of agriculture. On this occasion the media were present, including those from the United States. One afternoon I got a call from an American journalist of a world famous magazine. He said "Could I pay you a visit? Could you grant me an interview? I want to know more about banking in Luxembourg." I said, "Who gave you my name?" and he answered by giving the name of one of my friends at the U.S. Embassy in Luxembourg who, from time to time, was a sort of public relations man on my behalf. So the journalist and I made an appointment. He started by saying: "International banking and finance or economy are in general not my field. They are not my specialty. I usually cover political events, but I was at the European Center and the meeting lasted until the late hours of the night and nothing came out of it. So I don't know what to report and what to write about this meeting where for a reason, which I still don't know, my editor thought decisions would be made having an impact on agriculture in the United States as well. But, as I said, nothing came out of it. So I went to the U.S. Embassy and somebody told me—and that was my friend—that I should see you, that you have an open mind, that you lived in the United States during the war. Perhaps it would be interesting to hear from you about the human touch of banking and finance in Luxembourg."

I braced myself for questions I was not sure I could answer. But still I tried to make the best out of it, explaining at length and as clearly as I could what the Eurobond market meant for international banking, its origin and its implications, and so on and so on. He listened silently to what I said, but I did not perceive in his eyes a very great interest. He went on: "What is of interest to the readers of my column is the human aspect of banking in Luxembourg. You told me about the activities. So far so good. But could you tell me what kind of bankers you are in Luxembourg? Could you tell me whether they are young or old, whether they are of Luxembourg or foreign origin? I would also like to know a little bit more about the Luxembourg environment. How about night life? What type of night clubs do you have? And more particularly, what about restaurants? Are some of them listed in the Michelin Guide, with one or two stars?"

I was a bit hesitant before replying. Then I said: "Luxembourgers are an open-minded society. Therefore there are quite a number of foreign nationals working here." About night life, I didn't say very much for two reasons. First, I am neither an expert in this field, nor a regular visitor of the Luxembourg red-light district to which my wife would certainly not have given me the green light. On the other hand, I knew quite a lot about the restaurants in Luxembourg. I described the food, the specialties, and the atmosphere of a number of them. Relative to its size, Luxembourg harbors more restaurants of excellent quality than other cities. I concluded my comments by the phrase: "In Luxembourg, the bankers eat too much!"

A few weeks had elapsed after this interview. Then one day I found in my mail a copy of the magazine where the interview appeared. It was entitled: "Edmond Israel, a Luxembourg banker says: In Luxembourg, the bankers eat too much!"

I read this with slight misgivings. I thought to myself: "Is that all he retained from all the explanations I gave to him?" I also had an uneasy feeling: "How would some bankers from abroad react to this? Could this be detrimental to our center?" On the contrary. Beyond what I expected, this phrase attracted bankers to Luxembourg. Many called me, asked me about the environment in Luxembourg and if there is a good quality of living. The remark on the eating habits of the bankers in Luxembourg proved to be quite a hit. We were considered by many as what P.G. Wodehouse called "Good Trenchermen."

• Cedel/Clearstream

Somebody once told me, Edmond Israel has no children but he has Cedel. It appears that in the minds of people you are identified with that company which still operates out of Luxembourg with personnel of roughly 1,200 people but under the new name "Clearstream."

I am certainly not the father of Cedel. If you want to use that image, I would say that Cedel at least has two fathers: myself and the managing director of a large bank in Luxembourg with whom I had a chat one day in 1968 on the occasion of a business lunch. With my friend and colleague I periodically spoke about banking in Luxembourg, its possibilities, its future. On that specific day, we exchanged views again and we found that there is a great risk that activities linked to Eurobonds and other international financial instruments in general could slip away from Luxembourg finding other places, for instance Brussels. This would be the case if we would not rationalize the clearing and settlement of such transactions. The way this was handled since 1963 in Luxembourg was not only old-fashioned, but out of tune with the rapid growth of bond issues and secondary market transactions in these issues. The buyer had to settle by cash and then the transfer of the underlying securities took place by physical transport of these securities from one bank to another. It was a good business for package paper and cardboard boxes.

Let me recall here a rather amusing but also revealing story. When I made a presentation to the representatives of the Bankers Association composed of top managers, I suggested timidly that perhaps the time had come when we should wake up and find technical solutions in line with what the market demands as far as clearing and settlement is concerned. The top executives around the tables had different reactions. Some looked bored. It was clear to me how they thought: "This is just a technician's talk. Why did we invite him? He is a technical man. He should stick to his guns. We establish the strategy and we don't want to lose our time and be bothered by recommendations of a man who is not on our level in his bank." Others were a bit amused by the passion with which I developed my proposal. I overheard one of them whispering in the ear of his neighbor: "Well, I hope he's just as passionate when he returns home to his wife tonight." A participant at the meeting came up with a suggestion. He said: "We must buy a number of armored trucks, and the capacity of shipping the bonds from one place to another will have substantially increased."

Yes, that was the state of mind at that time. I do not want to criticize them. If today I would sit at a meeting, be on their level, and hear younger colleagues speaking of technological and intellectual innovations which appear on the market and which are just mind-boggling, I might very well think like them. Very often reactions are due to different kinds of mindsets linked to age or to old thinking.

I nearly forgot to tell you that in Brussels a new system for clearing and settlement had been set up by an American bank. The name of this system was and still is Euroclear. So, we not only had to act but to act fast. Quickly we founded a syndicate of study composed of a number of banks in and out of Luxembourg to draw up with the assistance of a well-known consultancy firm in Luxembourg a blueprint for a modern, up-to-date clearing and settlement system functioning electronically by computer.

To cut a long story short, we founded the company Cedel on September, 28, 1970, and the partner banks originated not only from Luxembourg but also from many countries in Europe, Asia, and even from the United States. Large banking groups were among the shareholders.

And how was this initiative received by the financial institutions active in the Eurobond market?

At the beginning with a lot of skepticism, even–and I repeat myself–with benign neglect and indulgent compassion. Who were we in Luxembourg to try to compete on the world market with institutions like Morgan Guaranty, which at that time operated Euroclear? The challenge was inspiring and the fight was quite tough. But we were supported by large banks which didn't want to leave this chunk of business to one of their major competitors, who would benefit from a monopoly in this field.

After the foundation of Cedel, I was elected chairman of its board, composed of over forty banks. During twenty years I was a non-executive chairman. So I did not take part in the day-to-day management. In principle the chairman was elected for a three-year term and the chairmanship should have been exercised on a rotating basis, but somehow this did not work out and the large banking groups preferred someone from a small country like Luxembourg to be at the helm of this institution. By the way, this is also often the case in politics, where Luxembourg acts as an intermediary and also conciliator in the world of economic and political competition.

So you consider yourself to have had a role similar to a statesman, a political leader?

Far from that, and if I give that impression by what I said, then I am sorry. Cedel is an international institution serving the market. Its influence and power do not go beyond that. After twenty years, I took the firm and irrevocable decision to resign after having found a top banker to succeed me who was retiring from his position as one of the leading executive directors of one of the largest banks in the United States.

Have you not any anecdotes to tell, amusing moments you have experienced?

Of course, quite a number. Some of them I don't remember in detail. Let me just evoke one rather funny event, which perhaps illustrates best to what extent during the first years of Cedel's existence it was quite unknown, except in the profession, and there again mostly in the sectors of the banks and brokerage houses dealing in international securities.

In a major capital of a European country, I chaired a press conference to describe Cedel to specialized newspapers and magazines. We sent out an ample number of invitations. Around me were sitting the members of the Executive committee composed of eleven banks and we were just waiting for the invitees. They were, let us say, drifting in. I started to welcome the representatives of roughly five to six newspapers and magazines. Among them there was a charming young woman. She was very attractive. Then we came to the questions. There were not too many. The last one came from the young female reporter. She said: "Well, Mr. Chairman, Cedel stands for what? I heard that you are in the ladies' fashion business, because I am representing a fashion magazine. I am surprised that this economic sector 'ladies' fashion' has developed in your country as a business on an international scope." I was taken aback by this question. When I saw the wide-open eyes of my colleagues, a smile came to my face and I said: "Miss, I thank you for this question. I shall speak to my wife. Perhaps it would not be a bad idea to start such a business in Luxembourg. For the time being, our business is clearing and settlement of international securities. Should you one day like to hear more about that, I am at your disposal."

This was just an episode on the lighter side of our activity. This activity grew considerably from year to year in parallel with the growth of the international capital market. As I said before, Clearstream clears at present more than 90 million transactions a year and holds in custody securities of about 8 trillion or 8,000 billion U.S. dollars. Clearstream is now wholly owned by Deutsche Börse AG, but its head office and operational headquarter are in Luxembourg. It has subsidiaries in London, New York, Tokyo, Hong Kong, and Dubai, and of course a major operational center in Frankfurt.

Are you concerned that the decision center is not in Luxembourg or exercised by Luxembourg as a majority?

I am a realist. I do not think that this is possible any more. By the way, multinational companies or multinational banks also become more and more international as far as their shareholder-ship is concerned. In the last resort, it boils down to one major challenge: offering top quality of services. If this challenge is met, it will be the key for success and even for continued success. We just have to be better and also in advance of others, to be among the top players in the league. This is the best guarantee for the future, also applied to our international banking center, where for more than forty years quite a number of promising activities have developed and matured.

This reflection leads to the some thoughts on the Luxembourg financial center in the future.

The role of banking in a fast-changing environment: Risks and opportunities for the future

Could you discuss your vision in this regard?

Yes, in a few moments. Let me however first, in order to conclude the part dealing with the origin and the development of the international banking center in Luxembourg, evoke the memory of a great personality on the political scene, Pierre Werner. He passed away in 2002 and undoubtedly has played a major role on the political and economic scene of Luxembourg in the postwar era. Luxembourg owes Pierre Werner an eternal debt of gratitude. Not only on the European scene has he laid down the groundwork of the European currency, the Euro. Furthermore, on the technological side, he had been the initiator and the promoter of the satellite company of S.E.S. ASTRA of worldwide scope, and last but certainly not least, he has been the father of the International banking and financial center. He had the vision of developing such an activity in Luxembourg since the end of the war. He transformed this vision into reality, first as finance minister and then as prime minister, establishing systematically and patiently a legal and regulatory framework coupled with a number of initiatives to foster this promising activity in Luxembourg. So, he's very often called the "father" of our international banking center. But Pierre Werner was a very modest man, a great man, and he always refused this title. He preferred by far to highlight and stress the merits and constructive role of others while remaining a little bit in the shadow, which was not really a shadow, because his personality was literally flooded in light, a light of a brilliant intellect, vast culture, deep religious feeling, and so many other talents in one single person. I had the privilege to know personally Pierre Werner very well, his beloved wife, and his children. For me, as for so many others in my country and also in other European countries, Pierre Werner will be and will remain a shining example.

Let's now turn to the future. How do you view the perspective for the sustainability of international banking in Luxembourg?

To stay or to remain with my metaphor, the curtain is still up and it must never come down, at least not in a foreseeable future. So, what do we have to do? The major trump in the stack of our cards is the fact that banking in Luxembourg has matured over the years and decades. I think this is very important and must be seriously considered. Otherwise, we become weak, because we are not sure of ourselves. Let me be very clear about that. To be sure does not mean to tout to the outer world that we are the best and the brightest. Such a language would be utterly wrong. It would be worse than wrong, it would be ridiculous. To be sure of oneself means sometimes to be soft spoken, to underrate things. To be, let me mention him again, like Pierre Werner. This was not the case when Luxembourg started as a banking center. We had to use a different language, but that was forty years ago. Facts must speak for themselves, and therefore we have to be factual when we speak to others, when we make conferences or participate in workshops.

Let me spell out some facts. First of all, the so-called "Feira Agreement." I think it was one of the most important steps and decisions initiated by our prime minister Jean-Claude Juncker and his close colleagues and collaborators, in order precisely not just to retain the banking secrecy, but also to assure to a large extent the sustainability of our banking center. It was an agreement which now is binding not only for the member countries of the European Union, but also *inter alia* for Switzerland. It provides a reasonable taxation of income, but also for the preservation of the confidentiality of bank accounts held in some countries like Luxembourg by residents and non-residents.

Then, there is a constant and rapid change in the types of activities exercised by the banks. We certainly must never think that we can or should do everything. In Luxembourg, most of the banks, mainly the larger ones, are of the universal type; in principle they are offering a wide spectrum of services. Yet their core activities are linked to private banking, and in its fold, the production and sale of a variety of instruments, such as investment funds, a sector in which Luxembourg plays an increasing role. Intellectual asset management in a variety of forms will be a very promising activity in the future. If Luxembourg engages itself in this direction, I think that this will constitute a major component of an increasing and rewarding activity in our specializations.

We must always strive to be better than others. Luxembourg already runs an International Banking School where many students and future bank managers, not only from Luxembourg but also from other countries, take courses. I think the Luxembourg banks, as well as the private sector in general, must engage themselves in an active cooperation with the University of Luxembourg and with institutions closely linked to it. Such cooperation must cover extensive research for the production of new instruments and the development of activities in specific areas. Thus Luxembourg will be a breeding ground of new types of operations, services, and products.

As we are multi-cultural and multi-lingual, this might help to give us a head start with regard to others. Finally, we must avoid equating quality of life with a comfortable mentality leading to complacency. Nothing is granted for ever and sustainability in success calls for constant efforts and innovation. We should never forget that man has to construct his future and not to submit passively to future trends and evolutions.

As Gorbachev said, "Life condemns those who are late." I would however like to add that "Life sometimes condemns those who are too early." To strike a balance between these two approaches will be our main challenge for tomorrow.

The heart and the mind

• Raymonde and Renée

After evoking your professional life both in the United States as a factory worker and then as a banker after your return to Luxembourg, what were the main events of your private life?

In 1949 my father passed away and in the following years the hand of five fingers had been successively amputated by another three fingers. My uncle David passed away in 1959, his wife, my aunt Clemy, died in 1961, and in 1963 I lost my mother. This was the shadow in my life. The light appeared with Raymonde, whom I married in 1958.

Raymonde had a light in her look. There was constant sunshine in her eyes. Her whole personality was radiant. She liked to laugh and when she looked at you, you just felt good, you felt a different person, and whatever worries you might have at that moment, they were dispelled. The French Jewish philosopher Emmanuel Lévinas once wrote in one of his remarkable books that "God is in the eyes of the other." That's exactly what you felt in the presence of Raymonde. As mentioned before, we married in 1958. That was rather late in my life. I was thirty-five years old. If it had not been for the exhortations of my mother, I probably would have remained a bachelor. I would have been lonely and in life there is hardly anything as tough as loneliness.

Raymonde was a very generous person. She was born in Alsace (France), where people have their feet firmly on the ground. They are realists, like the Luxembourgers by the way, and have a great sense of humor and a poetic vein. Like her father, to whom she felt very close, Raymonde was very fond of the Alsatian tales spiced with a particular sense of humor. When she laughed, her beautiful dark eyes were fiery, and at the same time smiling and gentle. She could never hurt a fly, certainly not a human being. To a certain extent, she was a bit introverted and her eyes succeeded in piercing the invisible but very solid armor of her personality. Like probably most women, if not all of them, she had a secret garden where she tenderly tended a flower. Her favorite flower was the forget-me-not, the "myosotis."

Raymonde was an excellent mathematician. She studied chemistry at the University of Strasbourg and worked there in a laboratory. After our marriage she gave up her profession. Perhaps at the beginning I did not realize what a sacrifice this was for her. When my uncle David passed away, she helped my aunt Clementine by visiting textile stores as a traveling saleswoman, doing this for several months until the demise of my aunt.

Contrary to me, a loner, Raymonde was very sociable and thanks to her we made quite a number of friends. In her presence people just felt good.

Raymonde was very sensitive and like many sensitive people, she was hurt in her life quite a number of times. She never showed it, but her soul was covered with bruises, the "bleus à l'âme" of Françoise Sagan.

In 1992 Raymonde was struck by cancer, the implacable disease which, like a Scottish shower, puts you into the darkness of despair and then again into a feeling of great hope, depending on the results of the x-rays or scanners. We fought together, Raymonde of course in the front line, and during four years we blessed every moment God or Destiny allowed us to be together. Finally, she passed away in 1996. There were around me many members of the family and friends, but I felt her absence every moment of my life, every day and night.

A few years later I met Renée at a dinner party of common friends. Again it was a stroke of luck, which I certainly did not deserve. But does one deserve luck? Sometimes it just happens. Physically, Renée is a striking beauty, blond hair, deep green blue eyes. Like Raymonde, she is generous, warm-hearted and very, very sociable. She has numerous friends.

At the dinner where we met, on the occasion of the seventieth anniversary of the birth of the host, I made a short speech, off the cuff. Her presence probably inspired me, and my speech left a deep impression with Renée, according to what she told me later. Before we parted from our host, I asked her spontaneously if we could meet again and just as spontaneously she answered, "Yes." We met several times and then I asked the traditional "Will you marry me?" and she answered after a few seconds of silence, "Yes." Fortunately for me I somehow pleased, if not all, but most of her friends. Their judgment concerning me was rather positive, but I think that Renée would have married me even if her friends' reactions to me would have been negative.

There is a difference of twenty-one years of age between us. In many respects, Renée and I are different. She is sporty and I do not practice any sport. She likes to have people around her and I very often feel comfortable being alone, alone with her. I have many anxieties and I show them. She also may have some, but without showing them. Yet we are firmly bound together. Our marriage is solid. It holds, contrary to the rather dire predictions of a number of our "friends." Some were gleefully waiting for the news of our separation. But this has not come and I don't think it will ever happen until the moment when the great

Separator will act. Renée is very insistent on keeping her own individuality, her own personality. After some quite lively discussions, each of us has gradually adjusted to the other. This is not an easy exercise, but once it is successful, I think this is highly commendable. In a couple of whatever age, to adjust and to adapt to the other is a necessity for the sustainability of marriage links.

Renée was very successful in business. Together with her younger sister, she managed a store, which belonged to her parents. She would indeed be successful in many other areas if the opportunity would be given to her.

On a strictly voluntary basis, after an appropriate training course, she is active in Luxembourg in the "Omega Group," consisting of people who assist the very seriously ill. Renée is an excellent psychologist and therefore quite successfully fulfills this job, which is more a vocation than a job. She listens more than she speaks to those who are ill and therefore they all are eagerly waiting for her next visit.

On March 17, 1999, we married at the Municipality of Luxembourg. The mayor of Luxembourg, Ms. Lydie Polfer, pronounced us man and wife in the presence of our close relatives and a limited number of friends.

We wanted also a religious marriage but not with all the ado's that surround such a ceremony in the small closely-knit Jewish community of Luxembourg. If you forget to invite somebody he will be angry, not his whole life, but perhaps for quite a number of years. My close friend Tony Cernera, president of Sacred Heart University of Fairfield, Connecticut, proposed to me to arrange a Jewish religious wedding in Fairfield with Rabbi Dr. Joseph Ehrenkranz, who has an office on the campus of Sacred Heart University. He is a conservative rabbi–or perhaps I should call him an enlightened orthodox rabbi–who has, together with Dr. Cernera, conducted interconfessional activities for decades in the United States. So the president of a

Catholic University, founded in 1963 by a bishop in Connecticut, arranged a Jewish religious marriage ceremony for his two friends from Luxembourg.

This is more then an interconfessional testimony, even more than a rare act of friendship. It is one of those manifestations giving a true meaning to marriage, a deep meaning to life. Renée and I are blessed by the friendship of Tony Cernera.

Speaking about Renée I become quickly excessive, even dithyrambic, which she doesn't like. So I confine myself to stress what it means to me to be married to her. Though I am already quite advanced in age, I learn a lot from her. After all, learning is a lifelong process. She taught me how to look at a painting. She has the gift to perceive instantly what the painter wants to express, either in figurative or abstract art. She somehow has the gut feeling for what is worthwhile or is better to be ignored. She has the same judgment in literature and music.

She likes to help others but hates to speak about it. She is never seen in the forefront and she does not like to be photographed by the media. The beauty of her soul matches her physical beauty.

I can't be anyone else than the one I am

Ego aliter quam sum esse non possum.
– Erasmus of Rotterdam

You have been raised in a very practicing religious family. But today, who are the great philosophers, theologians, or moralists who influence your thinking?

In the first place I would mention Erasmus of Rotterdam, one of the great humanists, because his vision collided with the conservative thinking of the Middle Ages. If I had to quote one of the great Jewish thinkers, it is certainly Maimonides (Moshe

Maimon), who lived in the fourteenth century. He paved the way for the future and so in his time did Erasmus of Rotterdam. Since my adolescence, I aspire to transpose in my daily life a philosophy based on ethics, which has to be enriched by enlightenment. That was precisely the essence of the thinking of Erasmus of Rotterdam.

Before we address the multiple aspects of your thinking, could you perhaps elaborate on the life of the Jewish community in Luxembourg, which was in the process of reconstructing itself after the war?

Right after the war, besides my professional work I engaged myself with great resolve and even enthusiasm in the Jewish community, where I assumed some functions of coordination in the field of cultural activities. I organized important conferences for the members of our community, featuring well-known personalities and thinkers.

In the late forties the Jews in Luxembourg, like their forefathers, lived culturally and religiously in a closed circle. They did not open up to the outside world. This happened only after the historic encounter of Pope John XXIII and the Jewish philosopher, Jules Isaac. When I was thirty-five years old, I was elected to be a member of the "Consistoire Israélite du Luxembourg," the board of trustees of the Jewish community. This was a record, because in the past only elderly people considered to be sufficiently mature became members of this entity. My first initiative consisted in inviting women to become members of the "Consistoire." My proposal met quite a lot of opposition, mainly by the diehards, who strongly believed that these functions belong exclusively to men. Some were openly hostile to such an idea, bordering for them on blasphemy. For a moment I felt like the Jewish philosopher Baruch Spinoza, fearing that I would be excluded from the community if not deprived of my status as a

Jew. It was a revolution. I felt in my innermost a deep satisfaction rather than mortification. Anyhow, nowadays it is considered as normal to include women in the lay management of a Jewish community. The present generation cannot even imagine that this could have been a problem some decades ago.

But let me evoke a more amusing happening.

Traditionally on our national holiday, a religious service is organized at the synagogue. On that occasion the president and the vice president of the Consistoire used to wear striped trousers with coat tails and a top hat. My financial resources at that time were rather limited and so I borrowed this attire from my uncle Max in Brussels. I looked a little bit like a Bavarian sausage because my uncle was slimmer than I. After the service the president and I, as vice president, accompanied the members of the government to the door. I overheard one of the ministers asking his colleague "A wien ass dat dann?" ("And who is this one?"). When I became President of the community, I abolished this attire which was not anymore up-to-date in the fast-evolving society.

A question of a more general nature: For centuries and centuries the Jews ask themselves questions about their real identity. There is the famous problem of the double, triple, or even more complicated multiple allegiance. Could you tell me what it is to be a Jew? What is Judaism? Is it a spiritual movement, a culture, a religion, a philosophy of life? What is it?

Frankly, I don't know too much. This question really never preoccupied me to a large extent. First of all, I never ask myself about my own identity. I am a Jew, I am a Luxembourger, I am a European, I am also an inhabitant of Planet Earth, the dimension of which appears to shrink more and more in the wake of a global network of communications. The multi-cultural identity is easier to assume by Luxembourgers than by people of other nations, except perhaps by the Americans. So for me, this famous problem of a double or multiple allegiance does not exist or is outdated. Being multi-cultural is indeed an enrichment because it permits human beings to have a broader and a deeper view on reality.

You asked me also "What is Judaism?"

I must say that in the last resort nobody has come up yet with a complete and satisfying answer. Since the Jews live as a minority in the Diaspora, they have been the object of many persecutions and many false accusations. Yet, unwaveringly they persisted in keeping their faith and their way of life. One finds them very often on the side of those who are persecuted. The Jews rank among the first defenders of human rights and yet it is an irony of history that those for whom the Jews fought with determination and conviction sometimes turn against them. An example is the reaction towards the Jews of part of the black community in the United States.

What really gave the Jews the strength to go on, not to despair and not to convert to other religions? What explains this phenomenon of survival throughout the ages? I think it is the unshakable faith in Life of the Jews. Judaism is a culture of Life. We raise our glasses of wine to Life. I know a prayer in which in a few lines the word "Chaim" (*Life*) appears at least ten times. The Jews have a passion for Life. They love Life passionately. In French, I call it "La vie, passionnément!"

If I understand you correctly, there is no clearly established definition of the Jewish identity.

Indeed, not *stricto sensu*. In my opinion one should speak rather of the Jewish phenomenon. Judaism is one of the numerous expressions of the human phenomenon, to quote the title of one of the works of the Jesuit theologian and scientist, Teilhard de Chardin.

In what manner is the Jewish expression of the human phenomenon different from others?

Here again I cannot deliver an exhaustive answer. I can only speak of what I feel by intuition. To give an illustration of how I sense Judaism, I would like to refer to an Italian movie picture I saw many, many years ago and which left on me an unforgettable impression. It is the Fellini film, *Nights of Cabiria*. Cabiria was a girl of loose morals, a prostitute, who was constantly abused by her pimps. She had been struck, she had been tortured, she had been sold to other men, she had been raped, and yet she kept an unshakable faith in the goodness of human beings. Cabiria indeed is the archetype of a human being, who only sees the good in man though she suffers from the evil. Yet she keeps hope. In that respect there is a profound analogy between the Jews and this woman whom, if I were a Catholic, I would call a saint. The Jew never deviates from the road he pursues throughout the ages, persisting in a deep conviction that in spite of all his sufferings, he should never give up and constantly look forward to better days, hoping and believing that tomorrow will be better than today.

If I understand you correctly, this is the famous "Prinzip Hoffnung," the Principle of Hope of the philosopher, Ernst Bloch.

Yes, but one must add another principle established by another Jewish German philosopher, Hans Jonas. It is the principle of Duty, to be followed in all instances of existence. A duty towards the other one, be it a member of one's own family, be it a neighbor, a friend or even someone unknown. One should constantly strive to help those who are in need or are treated with injustice. This is also why the authentic Jews are on the side of those who are mistreated and persecuted or who are living in the condition of an ethnic minority. The Jews throughout the ages have rarely been rewarded for this attitude, but it is not the reward which counts, but the innermost felt necessity to perform one's own duty.

You spoke about the Jews suffering from violence, persecution, discrimination. This is undoubtedly one of the greatest tragedies of history, but nowadays the state of Israel is adopting a much more combative attitude, judged sometimes as being excessively violent.

First of all it should be stressed that the state of Israel is the realization in our time of a two-thousand-years-old dream, the dream of the return of the Jews to Sion. The state of Israel was founded after the Holocaust and many survivors of this unprecedented tragedy in the history of humanity have found refuge in Israel. Right after the proclamation of the state by the United Nations in 1948, Israel was attacked from all sides. The Arab neighbors did not accept the idea of this state. But this time, contrary to the past, the Jews decided to fight for their own rights, for their existence. One should never forget that the foundation of the state of Israel has been approved by the vast majority of the members states of the United Nations in 1948. Since then, over a span of fifty years, Israel has been in a state of semi-peace and semi-war, sometimes in a state of war. It was under a constant threat. It is true that mistakes had been made by the successive governments of Israel. Nothing is always either black or white. The grey zone usually prevails in international relations.

But on both sides the younger generation, the generation of a new century will not and cannot accept a state of permanent violence, of sometimes harsh occupation on one side and terrorist suicide attacks on the other. With regard to the relations between individuals, particularly the young, there are many encouraging signs. Encounters and workshops take place, also in Luxembourg, involving the young Palestinians and Israelis. They want to build the future together, not based on mutual destruction but on constructive cooperation.

Let me refer to the Holocaust, to this expression of evil, which even the poet Dante or the painter Bosch could not have imagined in its dimension of unspeakable horror. You believe in God, you are a religious man. How can you reconcile the existence of God and this abysmal evil? A question which often has been asked in a rather provocative manner: "Can there be a God after Auschwitz?"

The question of evil is very difficult and complex, and has posed itself to man since he reached the so-called state of *Homo sapiens sapiens*. Indeed it is a very painful question, particularly for the Jews after Auschwitz. It is true that many religious Jews have vowed after the Holocaust not to set foot in a synagogue.

Does one have an answer to this question from a religious perspective? If I try to give an answer, it will only be fragmentary and slightly limping: God has given to man freedom of choice and when man chooses the road which is not illuminated by the commandments of ethics, there is a deep rift between the Creator and the creatures. The genocide and more generally the evil may be an expression of this fracture between God and humanity.

There remains however the problem of those who are innocent.

Indeed, the millions of Jews, Gypsies, and others who died in the Nazi camps were innocent. The same is true for all the children who go on dying in our time, victims of hunger, illness, wars, and genocides. They suffer the consequences of those who have chosen the bad road, but they are not the culprits. Why does God not intervene to prevent all this?

One cannot make God responsible of our faults, of our mistakes. To quote Teilhard de Chardin freely: "We have not reached the point Omega." We are still in a state of profound cosmic ignorance. For us, the ways of the Lord are impenetrable. This is the classic explanation of most of the religions.

I personally prefer another one: God has associated man in the process of creation, a permanent process striving towards perfection. When men deviate from the road leading to perfection by choosing the road of evil, this provokes mutual sufferings and God suffers with men.

Dialogue between all confessions and cultures

Before we approach the interconfessional dialogue, a theme which is very close to your heart, let us evoke briefly the Jewish religion. What is its essence, its fundamental principle?

Its essence is very simple and you as a Catholic will recognize it easily: "Don't do to others what you do not want them to inflict upon you." Two thousand years ago, one of our rabbis gave this reply to a Roman soldier, who asked him the same question. Indeed, the soldier asked for a very short and concise answer, lasting for only the time that he could stand on one leg.

This reply obviously recalls the message of Jesus.

Let us not forget that Jesus of Nazareth is born a Jew and his message "Love your neighbor as you love yourself" is enshrined in Judaism.

This similarity between the basic principles of Christianity and Judaism is an excellent prologue to conduct the dialogue between the two religions. Beyond certain theological differences, and even if some of them are important, the dialogue has an excellent basis.

Indeed the two religions are in agreement on what is essential: Love and respect of the other. If I engage myself with a lot of determination in the interconfessional dialogue, the main reason is that I consider this dialogue indispensable for the good under-standing among most human beings, in order to work for peace in our world. We all know the tragedies and the disputes which under the guise of religion have provoked fanaticism and a shock of civilizations in the past and even until today.

This dialogue took concrete forms in Luxembourg right after the war as witnessed by the creation of the Interfaith Association of Luxembourg. The dialogue with the Christian religion has allowed me to meet and to have affectionate links with outstand-ing persons like the Reverend Father Louis Leloir, a Benedictine monk of the Abbey Saint-Maurice in Clervaux, Luxembourg. He was a great scholar and I always admired his profound faith and his spiritual candor. I was sometimes invited to the abbey to share with the monks the fraternal Sunday meal. We all ate in silence without uttering a word. I also had the privilege to make a presentation at the cloister of the abbey on the history of the Jews in Luxembourg.

When Father Leloir was in Luxembourg City, he never failed to stay overnight in our home and, together with my late wife Raymonde, we had very profound conversations with him. It was always as if sunlight had entered our apartment, a light different from the one which comes from the sun, a light which goes straight to the heart. Father Leloir asked me often to lend him the keys of the synagogue, so that he could pray there. If asked why he went to the synagogue to pray the vespers, he answered with a kind gleam in his eyes: "I go to pray, where our Lord has prayed."

Let me also mention the active Jewish-Christian dialogue conducted for many years in the United States by Sacred Heart University, Fairfield, Connecticut under the enlightened guid-ance of its president, Tony Cernera.

Speaking about the interconfessional dialogue between the Christian and Jewish religions, don't you think that in our days other religions, in particular Islam, should be partners of this dialogue?

Without any doubt, but I think that beyond Islam and beyond other religions, we have to include in this dialogue also scientists and philosophers, discussing the basic principles which ensure peace and good understanding between the people of our planet.

In this context I strongly believe that we have to redefine what we mean by love: love thy neighbor, love the other. Love is multidimensional. In the relations between human beings of different creeds, cultures, and colors, the essential component of love is the respect towards the other. We must strive for social justice, but also in the relations between the individuals, show the other respect, never hurt her/his sensitivity, never inflict on her/him—be it done unwillingly—a moral wound.

This type of dialogue must be conducted as a way to construct the future together, rather than to evoke constantly the injustices suffered by many in the past. We must be engaged with resolve in the construction of a new world by New Thinking. This endeavor is particularly important in our time marked by globalization and instant communications. Each one of us, whatever his position in the society, whatever his geographical location, can be and should be an ambassador of dialogue.

Let me mention here the experience of ASEF, the Asia-Europe Foundation, which I believe is a good example. Founded in 1997, it is composed of the twenty-five member countries of the European Union, the European Commission as well as thirteen Asian countries. I represent Luxembourg on the board of governors of this institution. Since the foundation of ASEF, my personal contacts with the Asian cultures have been a great enrichment for me. I particularly appreciate the tactfulness, the natural attitude "never to have the other lose face" of my Asian friends, whatever their cultures, traditions, and religions are. Face-saving is the great lesson we, Occidentals, have to learn from our contact with Asians.

By applying the basic objectives of dialogue, we have to underline more specifically the necessity to construct together the future. We must lay the foundation of what I would call "global ethical standards." Atheists must be included in this dialogue. I personally think that in so far as a human being is engaged in the search of a fundamental reality and its meaning, he is in essence not an atheist. It depends on what you mean by God. I believe that Albert Einstein had a different concept of God than, for instance, the chief rabbi of Jerusalem. But both were religious in their personal philosophical thinking.

Let me repeat again: I am deeply convinced that global ethics have to be accepted by all as the key for a more just, a more human, and a more peaceful world.

What you refer to appears to me to be the "Weltethos" evoked by the Christian theologian Hans Küng. Do you really think that after the dramatic events of September 11, 2001 and the ensuing wars in Afghanistan and Iraq, that our world can find a common basis for such a dialogue and mutual understanding? The relations between the Occident and Islam are very strained. Furthermore, in the relations between the Churches and the so-called atheists, there is still a feeling of deep mistrust, because of the past injustices and persecutions which still linger in the minds of many people.

Indeed it is, as my friend Jean-François Rischard would call it, "High Noon." Time is of the essence to engage in the dialogue of the twenty-first century. In order to overcome the painful memories of the past, all of us–whether theologians, philosophers, scientists, or just people–have to be future-oriented in our thinking. We have to change our mindset. We have to build together a new world whose inexhaustible potential, not yet expressed in reality, invites us to action. This is my definition of a "New Thinking."

Part Three

New Thinking

The future is the promise of the dawn
inviting us
to create and to construct
rather than
to submit to the opacity of the unknown.

A new vision of the world

Reviewing the story of your life reveals a human being with a rather uncommon destiny marked by the love of life. This deep emotion runs like a red thread through all the stages of your life. Indeed it was the lifeline which allowed you to overcome all the perils and problems you were exposed to. This lifeline was nourished by an irresistible optimism and confidence in the future. In the face of a world where, since your birth until the inception of the twenty-first century, violence and conflicts are daily occurrences, could you tell me how you keep this optimism?

The way I see and feel it, optimism is more than an attitude in our existence. First it appears to me as a fundamental feature of our character, of our behavior programmed in our genes. Then as our existence unfolds, it is also a choice we make for the road on which we embark: Is it the one of pessimism and skepticism leading nowhere, except to failure? Or is it the one of confidence in the future, of viewing evolution as a dynamic process offering to man an infinity of opportunities? I definitely have chosen this latter road to meet the dangers and challenges life had in store for me. I also felt comforted in this approach by a philosophical conviction derived from the observation of the evolution of the universe.

Let me mention the example of life on planet earth. Since its start some four billion years ago, life–perhaps in accordance with some sort of a cosmic blueprint, which science has not yet unveiled–has evolved in a process of constantly increasing complexity and adaptation, leading to a phenomenon which might be defined as self-awareness and spirituality. Starting from the microorganisms, this evolution through countless phases, marked by trials and errors, has finally led to man, a species capable of reflecting on itself, on its destiny as well as on the universe of which it is part. If we don't destroy the biological phenomenon on planet earth, there is no detectable reason why this evolution should not go on, an evolution towards growing complexity and spirituality.

Ilya Prigogine speaks of the unidirectional arrow of time, only directed toward the future: there is no return to the past.

That's why fundamentally I am confident about the destiny of the human species, unless we destroy ourselves, which would be in the terminology of Prigogine a bifurcation leading to self-destruction. Naturally, there will be quite a number of dead-end-streets or dead-end-roads. But viewed globally, I am hopeful that humanity is embarked on the road leading to the ultimate point called by the Jesuit priest and philosopher, Teilhard de Chardin, the "point Omega," when man will merge with his creator, the ultimate and absolute reality. Expressed differently, it's through man, choosing the right road, that the fundamental reality is engaged in a process of permanent creation. If, on the contrary, we engage ourselves on the road of self-destruction, we shall fail. However civilizations similar to ours and existing on other planets of the universe might succeed in reaching the point Omega.

Do you think therefore that a new planetary thinking will be the main and important milestone on this road leading to ultimate accomplishment?

We do not live in a deterministic world such as some physicists, like, for instance, Laplace, have postulated in the past. Destiny is not a fatality but a potential offered to man. He uses it or he doesn't; either he is conscious that reality is a dynamic process or he remains static, past-oriented and that leads to destruction. Man has the freedom to choose. He is the master of his destiny. But he must be guided in his steps. He must take an orientation consistent with some kind of a blueprint unveiled progressively through the discoveries of science and the philosophical implications. This planetary thinking could be described as philosophical software programmed for a new attitude of man in his behavior and his relations with others, be it on an individual scale or on the scale of peoples and cultures.

Aware of the difficulties which always arise when fundamental changes occur in the society, I would like to propose the following approach.

First a new vision of our world, or should I call it a new world view as science presents it to us at the present state of knowledge. This new view should necessarily lead to a new mentality, a new frame of mind, which again will lead to a new behavior in the relations between men. These three elements are entangled together. They are the building blocks for a better society in the twenty-first century.

The scientific work and philosophical considerations by Ilya Prigogine have inspired me in those reflections.

It would perhaps be interesting to speak briefly about Ilya Prigogine, a scientist and philosopher of science whom you like to quote.

It is a fact that I have a lot of admiration for Ilya Prigogine, who has been a real source of inspiration for me. Both scientist and philosopher of science, he has achieved a combination of these two approaches which cannot be separated anymore in the twenty-first century. In the last fifty years, particularly in physics and astrophysics, more progress has been made than in the last two thousand years. By speculating on the essence of what we, at present, perceive as reality, I believe that theoretical science cannot be ignored. Philosophizing in a speculative manner without referring to what science reveals to us today, is just an exercise in some sort of vague mumbling and confused verbosity. Authentic scientists, explaining their findings to those who are interested but who do not have the possibility to follow them in the mathematical formulation, are very clear in their communication. It was definitely the case as far as Ilya Prigogine is concerned. Based on his scientific research on the second law of thermodynamics, he introduced the notion of a deterministic chaos. He earned the Nobel Prize through his work on the biological phenomenon which arose on our planet in what he called "dissipative structures" of self-organized systems. It is the phenomenon of "neguentropy" versus entropy. He also postulated that time is an irreversible dynamic process. The arrow of time is only pointing in one direction: forward! But the bifurcations where these self-organized systems arise cannot be predicted. They can only be anticipated on the basis of probabilities. Indeed it is what Prigogine called "the end of certainties."

Thus, Prigogine postulates that reality is a permanent construction. It evolves, it is unpredictable, and at the same time is irreversible. The arrow of time therefore is in one direction only.

In substance, your conclusions are based on these three fundamental principles: continuous creation, an unpredictable evolution, and time which is irreversible. How do you relate your planetary thinking to these principles?

They lead to a new vision of the world, which implies three consequences:

1. Nothing is permanent, but change. Our world is not static but dynamic. Creation is not a unique original act but a continuous process. Man at the present state of intellectual and spiritual evolution is called upon to be an active participant in this process.

2. The potential is richer than the real. The future is wide open. It is an infinite dimension of potentialities. It is up the human species to seize them or not.

3. The arrow of time points in one direction, the future. The past is irreversibly over. It is useless and even detrimental to regret it or to attempt to reestablish it.

At first sight, this vision of the world appears elementary. In reality it is not. We only have to think of the countless fatalists and pessimists surrounding us, not to speak of the fundamentalists and integrists of all sides and directions. They are rooted and rigidly fixed in ancestral traditions and thinking belonging to the past. They deny all forms of progress and change, and their actions lead inexorably to conflicts and violence, such as terrorism on our planet.

Thus a new vision of the world calls for a new sense of responsibility of men. We must reach a new level of maturity in our thinking and in our actions. We must be the builders of the future where man will live globally in a society of justice, in a society of peace, where prosperity will no longer be exclusively reserved to a minority. This of course calls for new standards in ethics, to which I shall revert in one of the following chapters. The point I want to make now is: This is not utopian, but a compelling necessity of survival for mankind.

Based on science, if I understood you correctly, your reflections do not appear to have a religious connotation.

I do not see here any contradiction or incompatibility. On the contrary. In the first chapter of Genesis, there is a beautiful description of man feeding himself at the tree of knowledge. Acquiring knowledge is one of the most fundamental commandments. Acquiring knowledge is not a static exercise but a dynamic process. In our time we speak of lifelong learning. Learning what has been written and expressed in the past has to lead man to create and communicate new knowledge by engaging himself on the infinite road of new discoveries and ultimately to wisdom. Let me illustrate this by a dialogue I imagined between a religious man and a philosophical physicist.

Dialogue between a religious man and a philosophical physicist

RELIGIOUS MAN: *Descartes said: "I think, therefore I am!" I say: "I believe, therefore I am!"*

PHILOSOPHICAL PHYSICIST: As a scientist, I do not see any contradiction *a priori*. To believe and to think are the inherent qualities of man conscious of his existence.

But there is a whole universe between believing and thinking. Thinking is a rational exercise to analyze established facts. To believe is an act of faith. When I say I believe in God, in a Supreme Being who created the universe and who acts in it, I draw my conviction from the Holy Scriptures, which have been transmitted to us and which I consider as the eternal truth. When I pray, I sense the proximity of God and without seeing Him nor understanding Him, I feel His presence both transcendental and immanent.

On this last point, I am not so distant from you. The awe which I feel when I make a discovery must be very similar to the mystical elevation which you experience in your intense prayer. Don't forget that reality is a whole, encompassing both the visible and invisible; matter and spirit are entangled. For some of us physics lead to metaphysics.

This is possible, but as a physicist, you draw your certainties from science. Well, science will always reach limits. You miss the essential: what is beyond this limit, the Absolute.

You are right: science cannot prove or disprove the existence of God. Science reaches irreversibly a point, let us call it a wall. Everything that is situated beyond this wall is a matter of pure conjecture. Heisenberg, one of the founding fathers of quantum mechanics, speaks in this context about "steps beyond frontiers." Thus I shall never know the absolute truth, but at the same time I shall relentlessly search for this truth. The search for the absolute gives to man a sense of fulfillment and joy.

All this does not mean that there is no convergence between us. The laws of nature and the universal constants, such as the law of gravitation, leave a wide-open field of interpretations in which the believer and the scientist can meet and conduct a constructive dialogue. Are the laws of nature the product of coincidence or is there an underlying principle which we have not yet discovered? In the framework of the theory of chaos, scientists, particularly Prigogine, have identified a chaos which is not entirely contingent and which marks a tendency of self-organization. The believers see there the hand of God, while the researchers, as strict scientists, ask themselves feverishly what is behind this mystery of a self-organizing principle.

Albert Einstein did not practice his religion but he was penetrated by the idea that the universe itself had a meaning, based on the laws and principles, determining fundamental reality. Others, like Paul Davies, speak of a "cosmic blueprint and the mind of God." Wolfgang Pauli, a Nobel Prize winner in physics, mentions the soul of the world: "anima mundi." Some scientists are deeply religious, like the Pakistani Muslim physicist Abdus Salam, who received the Nobel Prize with Steven Weinberg and Sheldon Glashow. He prays three times a day; at the same time he is a passionate researcher. He feels no contradiction in this. The Koran recommends to the faithful to study and to understand the laws of nature.

Thus, are you identifying the basic principles and laws with God?

As a physicist, I do not attach any specific name to a reality or non-reality, which is beyond the field of my scientific explorations. But let me mention here the ancient Hebrews, who had an astounding insight, one of the commandments of the Decalogue stating not to make an image of God. The Jews not only refrain from a given picture of God, but they also don't name Him. There is one exception: On the day of Yom Kippur, the most sacred day in the Jewish calendar, the High Priest entering the Holy Arch, pronounces loudly and clearly the name of God. But on Yom Kippur the Jews for twenty-four hours live in a spiritual dimension, detached from space and time. In the Holy Scriptures, a multiplicity of names defines what man perceives as an emanation of the divine manifestation.

If I interpret you correctly, in your vision as a scientist, there is no opposition between faith and science, between spirituality and scientific research. Thus, science and faith are complementary. When science reaches its limits, it leaves the field of the absolute to the believer.

Not exactly. I rather see the two roads followed by the believer and the scientist as parallel. The believer in his exercise of meditation and contemplation tries to deepen and to give continuously a new sense to his faith, while the scientist in the exercise of research and exploration attempts to widen constantly the field of the knowledgeable. By walking down these two roads, the two, the believer and the scientist, follow a common mysterious and irresistible urge anchored in the human species: the search for absolute truth. They attempt to reach the same ultimate goal by different, parallel approaches. At the end of time, they will meet in the discovery of absolute truth.

Would that be the point Omega of Teilhard de Chardin?

If you wish, but as a scientist I prefer to speak of all the parallels which ultimately will meet and merge. In the meantime nothing prevents the physicist to believe and nothing prevents the believer to engage himself on the road of the philosophical scientist, contemplating and studying the laws of nature. The Jewish rabbi and philosopher, Alexandre Safran, in his work *The Wisdom of the Kabbale*, expresses a beautiful and deep thought: "To the extent that science progresses in its constant evolutionary process, man gets nearer to the divine light."

In my own philosophical interpretation, science is universal and fulfills a unifying role, a role of reconciliation and pacification between the oppositions which divide humanity. It thus fulfills an important function, aiming at eliminating ancestral and contemporary oppositions.

Two roads, same destination

Mr. Israel, there's a question I've wanted to ask you for quite some time: You obviously have a certain preference for physics and the physicists. There is, however, in the scientific heritage, in particular of the nineteenth and the twentieth century, a vast array of important scientists of other disciplines inviting us to philosophical reflection, in particular Darwin, as well as Watson and Crick, who discovered the intimate structure of the human genome with all its therapeutic and sociological and philosophical implications.

I cannot deny that I have a certain predilection for fundamental physics and physicists, because their field of research touches on the infinite both in its macro and micro expressions. They knock at the door of the Absolute. The biologist or biochemist, for instance, deals with life on our planet, a rather recent phenomenon compared to the birth of the universe. They rationally analyze the functions and mechanisms of the biological systems in their evolutionary process. Many of them claim that these self-organizing systems can be explained without having recourse to an all-overarching divine principle. Richard Dawkins speaks of the "Blind Watchmaker."

Personally I am fascinated by physics and cosmology, which from a philosophical point of view strike a chord in my own deep quest. I read years ago that some serious scientists were asking themselves whether there still remained something to discover in physics. I found this very strange and in complete contradiction to my own thinking. I am convinced that in physics and in cosmology, there is an infinity of concepts and manifestations to be discovered. The search will go on and on and on until the end of time. And that's why I think that this field of human exploration and search will lead us continuously to new insights, new discoveries, to an intense feeling of fulfillment and awe, a link to the Absolute.

The philosophical scientist concludes the dialogue with the believer insisting on the universal and unifying role of sciences in our time. How do you view this role of integration?

On the scientific level, the discoveries constantly bring new insights, new knowledge which will exert an influence on our way of thinking, on our way of understanding the other and also on our beliefs. In the past, since antiquity, scientists have made important discoveries. These were reserved to an inner circle, and their communications to the outside usually never extended beyond the local or regional sphere. The vast majority of human beings was not informed and did not feel concerned, and therefore in their own thinking remained static. New insights and new knowledge were calling for change, but most of the people had no access to the progress of knowledge, thus remaining entrenched in their past thinking.

Today, in line with the extraordinary progress made in the acquisition of knowledge, science has gained credibility and authority. Research is growing exponentially. That is the positive result of globalization. In our increasingly interconnected world, new knowledge is communicated and accessible to everyone wherever he lives. Therefore I think that man should necessarily be influenced in his belief and in his ideology by this new world image which is unveiled to us by science. Believers, atheists, scientists, and philosophers contribute to building a universal platform of knowledge, which in a compelling manner will sooner or later lead to new thinking, planetary thinking. Such thinking is essential in a number of areas where the very existence of humanity and life on our planet are threatened. And here I single out the demographic explosion, the heating of the planet, the destruction of ecosystems, just to mention these few deadly risks.

I am hopeful and confident but not sure that a new planetary consciousness will gradually emerge and translate itself into more responsible behavior and a greater solidarity of humanity. Obviously, this cannot be realized in a single day. I am convinced that man in the twenty-first century, alongside his attachment to his country of origin and to his regional culture, will feel himself more and more concerned with the destiny of the human beings and he will also demonstrate an increasing attachment to the blue planet that is his home. In the last instance, as I said before, it is a matter of the survival of the human species on our planet.

In what manner could this unifying role of science influence the believer in your dialogue? More fundamentally, what will be the impact of this universal platform of self-imposing scientific evidences on the beliefs, convictions, and religions of people in our time?

It is up to each one to rebuild his personal philosophy on the basis of this common scientific platform. Still largely divergent at present, religious beliefs and convictions can no longer be in fundamental opposition to knowledge. In our time, immediate communications should lead to a common vision of the universe and this is a positive point.

I do not think that this evolution will result in a universal religion. The quest toward the Absolute, toward the fundamental reality, will manifest itself in multiple ways illuminated by the dazzle and awe of the scientists and the fervent prayers of the believers.

But there is a second point, a very important one: global ethics. I have already evoked this essential point in a preceding chapter dealing with the dialogue among all confessions and cultures. A new planetary consciousness rooted in universally recognized scientific discoveries with philosophical implications will shape not only new thinking but a new, more responsible behavior in the interest of humanity as a whole. Deviating from this path of planetary responsibility would lead inexorably to the disappearance of the human phenomenon from our planet, as illustrated by the dangers of the warming of the planet, a continuous demographic explosion, wars, and terrorism, with their corollary of hunger, misery, and desperation experienced by billions of people.

Before approaching the last chapter showing some possible ways to reach all these goals, let me illustrate by a few short stories some of the imperfections, injustices and flaws of our society in our time.

A perfectible society in short stories

For the sake of philosophy

The meeting was over earlier than anticipated, and the banker went to the bar of his hotel, situated on the last floor. The place was rather deserted at this time of the afternoon. Wanting to find some moments of solitude and relaxation, he ordered a double scotch with ice and soda while his thoughts were migrating in all directions.

A young woman in tight jeans underlining the shape of her body entered the bar. She cast a quick glance around her and finished by looking at the banker. She approached the table and asked if she could take a seat. The banker was taken aback because the bar was practically empty. He quickly said yes and asked whether she would like to drink something. She ordered a cola light.

Smiling, she engaged in conversation right away:

"May I ask where you are coming from and what you are doing? I suppose you are on business?"

"Yes. I come from Europe and I am a banker. And you, what are you doing?"

"I am a 'walking girl.' "

"A walking girl? And you walk like this the whole day?"

"No, only in the afternoon and in the evening."

"Where? In the street?"

"No, I walk from one bar to another."

"But for what reason?"

The young girl appeared surprised. She sipped her cola and said:

"In order to finance my studies."

"Your studies?"

"Yes, I am a student in philosophy and once I have completed my studies, I want to become a professor. But in the meantime I have to cope with my finances, which are limited. You know universities are very expensive in this country, especially those who rank among the best. Since it is not easy to find a job, in particular a well paid job, I decided to become a 'walking girl.' "

"Well! To use a word from the philosophical vocabulary of the ancient Greeks, you are a peripatetic, a street walker or should I say bar walker?"

The girl, a bit astonished said:

"Oh, you seem to be quite familiar with philosophy! That is not so common for bankers. I believe that we are made to understand each other. By the way, you are right: the name given to the women who exercise my profession derives from the Greek 'peripatetic,' the disciples of Aristotle who philosophized while strolling on the boulevards of Athens. But did you know that these ancient philosophers in Greece did not walk for their pleasure, but by necessity?"

"Frankly no. I ignored this . . ."

"They were walking because of a lack of means to cover the rent for a special place where they could dispense their teaching to others. So I feel close to them because of my own financial problems, but I have one single goal: to obtain a Ph.D. in philosophy, and I shall succeed in spite of my difficulties of the moment. And I shall be a university professor, I shall start a family with a man who will love and respect me, and we shall have children."

"You are an optimist. You believe that in spite of your past as a peripatetic, you will be engaged by a university. You must be very naïve."

"I am convinced of that. Our society is full of hypocrisy and is calling for a change. If you take a look at the cover pages of a number of magazines, if you look at so many movies, if you look at the so-called respectable women of the upper classes, they are wearing clothes which uncover more than they cover. They want to look enticing and sexy, whether they are young or old, whether they are pretty or ugly. We, the street walkers, the prostitutes, how can we distinguish ourselves from them? Surely not through our clothes anymore. I think that we should describe our job in a different manner."

"What do you mean by that?"

"I just mean that we are therapists. We bring healing and consolation to those who are lonely, to those men who are ugly, to those men who cannot find a companion, as well as to those who are frustrated by the attitude and the remarks of their partners. So they come to us. We are paid, rather underpaid, to bring consolation and solace to all these sick and unfortunate people. And you see that for all these reasons, my dear banker, I believe that I shall succeed."

"Listening to you, I am sure of this, because you are intelligent and know what you want. In any case, I wish you good luck with all my heart. May I offer you another coke or something else?"

She looked at her watch.

"No thanks. I haven't time anymore. But if you wish we can pursue our conversation in your room. I charge one hundred dollars per hour, but as I like you, I grant you a reduction: fifty dollars, for the sake of philosophy."

The banker thought for a moment. It was not the cost which made him hesitate, but the moral inhibitors firmly encroached in him, his principles, and his reputation.

She perceived his hesitation and anticipating his refusal, she got up.

"Sorry, I have to continue my long march. I have not yet earned a single dollar today and my dues have to be paid by the end of the month. Thanks for the coke. Until some other time, perhaps . . ."

She gets up from the table and leaves the bar rather precipitously.

The banker did not expect such a quick departure. He was asking himself whether he should not have accepted her invitation, or at least given her fifty dollars, just like that? Without any strings attached, for the sake of philosophy?

Abruptly he got up from his chair and nearly fell over a stupefied barman: "Excuse me. I'll be back in a moment." He ran to the elevator, his portfolio in his hand:

"Miss, wait a second!"

Too late. The elevator had already started its long descent to the ground floor.

For the sake of science

It was a hot, sweltering summer day. Crossing the park, the student, though young and fit, was suffering from the heat and constantly wiping the perspiration from his face. He saw a bench and dropped down on it. Then he saw a small old man approaching the bench. The man had red cheeks, was amply perspiring, and out of breath. He quickly glanced to the right and left, and before taking a seat, he asked politely:

"May I?"

He was so exhausted that he could not wait for the answer. Breathing heavily, he practically fell down on the bench. His attire was rather conventional, and in spite of the heat he wore a black suit with a yellow tie and a shirt which once upon a time was white, but on that day was wet and wrinkled. He wore a straw hat which probably dated back to the Roaring Twenties. He was carrying a leather brief case bursting in all corners. The old man was trying to regain his breath.

The student:

"Are you alright, sir?"

"Yes, yes . . ."

The man was one of these old people who even if they look very ill do not want compassion. They still have the illusion that they are alright and much younger than they look or are. The man went on:

"You know it's the heat, just the heat!"

Carefully he put the briefcase on the bench besides him as if it would contain all the valuables of the world.

The man repeated again:

"What heat! It's not common here in Luxembourg."

The student did not really want to engage in conversation. He nodded and plunged into the text of the chemistry course he had taken in the morning. He noticed that the old man surreptitiously looked over his shoulders. He did not mind. After all, the old man would not understand anything about it.

The man:

"Sorry, to interrupt you again in your review of your course. According to what I saw, you are a student in organic chemistry. May I ask a short question, if this doesn't trouble you very much?"

The student, surprised by the knowledge of the stranger, nodded affirmatively.

The man:

"In fact, I only wanted to know whether your studies give you satisfaction."

The student was somehow surprised and, ignoring the identity of his neighbor, preferred not to open up too much to him. He said:

"I chose this discipline because I thought it is fascinating, in particular in biochemistry and genetics. But the way the courses are presented to us could be more interesting."

"Don't worry, I ask you this question for my own reasons. I was a professor in physics, but a long time ago I retired. I understand what you mean. You feel disappointed!"

"Yes, I am disappointed. It's deadly boring. Our courses stop when really they should become interesting. Instead of concentrating on contemporary science or the latest discoveries which mark our time, our courses deal essentially with the history of science. Thus there is little time left for the passionate field we would like to explore with our professors: how the present-day research leads to undoubtedly fascinating discoveries in the future. Only few think how interesting a modern up-to-date course in chemistry could be. It's unbelievable . . ."

"I share your view. You know, after my retirement, I registered as a free student in various courses, particularly astrophysics and cosmology. The reason is not only to remain active but also to discover in the present state of knowledge a new holistic image of reality. But very soon I gave up. It was really deadly boring. What we learned in these courses was indeed light years away from present day scientific research. So I quit and decided to write a book. Even if nobody reads it, for me it was a relief, to express my innermost feelings, a vision inspired by contemporary scientific research. You know, Mr. Student, paper is the most patient material on earth. Think about the myriads of worthless reflections, of worthless musical notes and worthless paintings put on paper, but paper submits to it willingly as it does to my phantasms and mental vagrancies."

"It is really reassuring to hear you say all this. It confirms what I dimly perceived all the time. I am sorry that you have retired. I would have been delighted to attend your courses."

The old man took a certain time before he replied:

"You know, my young friend, during my active life, I thought in the same way as your teachers do. I was conscientious; I prepared my courses with great care, and gave quite a number of explanations whenever asked. When I returned to the university as a student after my retirement I realized the failings and flaws of a methodology as it is consigned in the text book. During my active life, without being conscious of it, I was teaching the past, I was a historian of science."

"I am sorry. I did not want to embarrass you . . ."

"Don't apologize. I have overcome this shock. To realize that many of my colleagues made the same observation, gives me a lot of comfort. Let me mention here what the Nobel Prize winner, Pierre-Gilles de Gennes, had written in one of his books. He recalls the boring manner in which chemistry was taught to him in the lycée (*high school*). This induced him, once he became known worldwide and therefore credible, to voluntarily teach a few lessons in contemporary chemistry in the high schools of France in order to convey a new image of science in our time and to provoke enthusiasm among the students.

And that's how the idea to write a book on today's science arose in my mind. I had also some contacts with the Institute of Santa Fe in New Mexico, where well-known scientists in different disciplines–physicists, astrophysicists, biologists, chemists, mathematicians, sociologists, psychologists, and so on–work together in exploring the basic principles applying to all sciences and based on a new holistic paradigm: complexity and adaptation in the evolutionary process. This book took me ten years to write, but far from hard work, it proved to be a most stimulating and exhilarating exercise. Scientific research is progressing at such a fast pace that each time I thought I had come to a valid conclusion, I had to revise and correct what I had written. I am now on my second revision already. In substance, what I want to communicate to the teachers is that in their courses they must never be static in their thinking. In their teaching they must give priority to new theories leading to new discoveries. Then they will succeed at instilling in the mind of the students a feeling of enthusiasm and fascination. But in order to achieve that, the teachers have to be themselves enthusiastic."

"Is your book on sale in bookstores already?"

"Not yet. I just got a first print from my editor, and I have it here with me."

The old man pulled a large volume from his briefcase and nimbly turned some pages as if he would be caressing and stroking a beautiful woman. Then with a generous gesture, he handed over this book to the student and said:

"I take pleasure in giving it to you. You will be my first reader."

Feeling some hesitation in the eyes of the student, he added:

"Don't worry. You don't owe me anything. It's a gift for the sake of science."

Condemned to die:
The judge and the inmate of Death Row

The old solitary judge, who never wanted to admit either to himself or to others his age, was condemned to death, not by justice but by the medical field: "In view of the advanced state of the tumor I owe you the truth. Nothing can be done anymore, even surgery would be useless." That's what he has been told by his doctor. On the judge's question of how much time was left to him, the doctor after a brief hesitation answered: "Based on my experience, six months, perhaps a bit more, perhaps a bit less. I am sorry for you."

During his professional career, the judge had pronounced quite a number of death sentences. In the judiciary, he was called "Old Sparky." His sentencing was based on the principle that those who willfully and deliberately commit murder, take the life of others, do not deserve to live themselves, and therefore are to be sentenced to death. He was heavy-handed but had a quiet conscience.

But when he saw himself put in the "Death Row" by the medical profession, the judge did not understand this. He always had done his duty. He rarely missed a religious service on Sunday. He had been an irreproachable spouse. What happened to him now must be a terrible mistake, a judicial mistake, and since the medical world did not know the procedure of the appeal, the sentence by the medical doctors handed out to him was without appeal. There is no Supreme Court of Medical Justice. How can he go on living, even a single day, with such a mental stress?

In his desperation, he suddenly recalled the case of Peter M. condemned to death by one of his colleagues for rape and murder. Peter M. always claimed to be innocent. He might be able to give him some comfort under the tragic conditions he undergoes now himself.

After many contacts he made with highly-placed persons in the judiciary and penitentiary, he finally succeeded in obtaining the authorization to meet and to speak to Peter M.

Peter M. is an African-American, born in a poor family, living a miserable existence under dire conditions. As a child, he proved to be quite intelligent, but he was brought up without any love and affection. He never had a chance in his life. After having left school, he was continuously jobless and started to commit minor misdemeanors. And then, one day, he was arrested for rape and murder. He admitted the rape but always denied vehemently the charge of murder. He pretended that he only raped the woman and left her alive in a backyard and that someone else must have killed her. He was badly defended by a court-appointed lawyer. This is very often the case for those who are living on the fringes of society. He was condemned to death and from procedure to procedure, he awaits his execution for more than ten years, locked up in the place called "Death Row."

This is the background of the two personalities who meet one day and start a conversation in a prison.

Peter M., a stocky man, his face marked by the life in prison, approaches slowly and heavily the iron screen separating him from his visitor. In a tired and aggressive voice, he addresses himself to the judge:

"My lawyer told me that if I agreed to speak to you, you could possibly help me for the review of my trial."

"Who tells me that you are really innocent?"

"But I am, it's just like that. I swear it on the head of my mother, on the Bible, on everything you wish. I never killed anyone. My condemnation is a scandal. Nobody has any proof

against me. But if you don't believe me, we have nothing to say
each other. There is a certain time for me to live. I can't lose time
in idle and useless conversations. Get out of my sight! I don't
want to see you any more!"

Peter M. gave a signal to his guards to take him back to his cell.
The Judge:

"But wait! Let's suppose that you are innocent. Personally I
am willing to believe you. After all, it was not I who condemned
you, but even if I wished, I'll have neither the possibility nor the
time left to me to do something for you."

"But you have influence. And you are retired. You have all
the time to help me if you wanted to do that."

"You are mistaken. Like you I am also condemned to die. I
have an incurable cancer."

"Well, that's sad for you, but it doesn't concern me."

"According to what the doctors say, my days are numbered.
I wanted just to ask how you endure this feeling, being
condemned to die very soon. After all, we both share the same
destiny. You, condemned by the human judiciary, and I, by the
human medical profession. Both of us, innocent and condemned
to death, we must have something to say to each other."

Peter M., numb, bewildered and speechless doesn't react for
several moments. Then he explodes:

"You are shit! You talk crap! Aren't you ashamed of yourself?"

Peter M. is shouting furiously, menacing the judge by shaking the iron screen.

The guards rush in the direction of the condemned man and
put shackles on him to bring him back to the cell.

But the judge stopped them:

"Please, leave him alone. I have to speak to him. It's indispensable and I have the authorization."

Peter M. hesitates. As he hates the guards even more than he
does the judge, he finally agrees to sit down again, and proceeds
more calmly:

"Listen, Old Sparky! How do you dare to compare yourself to me? I have never killed anyone. And you? You have tens and tens of human lives on your conscience!"

"I only did my duty. I applied the law."

"That's it. You apply the law and you even have a good conscience. For me, it's just murder what you did."

"Listen . . . Peter, I don't allow you to . . ."

"Excuse me! But of the two of us, the innocent, that's me! And if one of us deserves the death sentence, it's you. You have killed or you induced others to kill, not I. Are you religious, Mr. Judge?"

"Of course."

"OK, but I am not. God has deceived me. I have no confidence in him anymore. I know the fifth commandment: "Don't kill!" (*Thou shall not kill*). This commandment doesn't allow any exception."

"Frankly, I am not a theologian; I apply the law, which I swore to apply when I took office."

"Listen to me, Mr. Judge. This discussion will lead us nowhere. I know now that you cannot save my life. All I wish is that my sufferings will finish as soon as possible. Look at my hair. It is white and I am not even thirty years old. Try to imagine just for a moment my anxiety in the evening each time when I go to sleep, and I don't know whether I shall still be alive in the morning. To leap up in my slumber and to jump out of my bed when I hear steps on the floor in the corridor. Frankly I can't go on anymore. I don't want to live anymore. Lets get it over as soon as possible."

Several months later, at dawn, Peter M. jumps out of his bed when the guards wake him up. He knows that the moment has come.

He is trembling, he is shivering, he fights, he shouts. He asks for a pardon. In this last fight he doesn't want to give up a life which was so miserable for him. The guards put shackles on him and bring him by force to the place of execution. They place him on a stretcher, his hands and feet firmly bound with ropes which bite into his flesh. Peter M. takes a deep breath, shuts his eyes and when the lethal injection is given to him, he sees at the end of a dark corridor a white light, a light brighter than a million suns, a flooding light which takes him away, very far away.

The same night, the old judge dies in his sleep in the hospital. In his slumber, he has torn off all the tubes, his last lifeline.

Julius asks questions

Julius is a bright, young boy, very curious, and asks his parents questions all the time. They feel drowned in a sea of questions; they try to answer to the best of their knowledge.

Here are some samples of questions, which of course change with Julius's age.

Julius: Could you tell me why on the publicity for cars or for frying pans, there are very often nude women?

Father: To draw more the attention to the publicity and the items on sale.

Oh yes? But why not nude men

I have to think about this.

* * * * *

On television or on photos in the press it's funny to see the heads of states or the heads of governments, when they meet each other: they slap themselves on their shoulders or in the back. What does that mean?

I think that in politics, which is all a matter of nuances, these slaps on the shoulders should show that one has particularly warm and friendly relations with the colleague of the other country. If politicians only shake hands, that definitely signifies that the relations have become slightly colder.

*   *   *   *   *

Pop, you make me take courses at the academy of music. I was able to appreciate the works of your favorite composers, like Bach and Beethoven. But could you tell me what do rock and hard rock mean to you?

For me, they are expressions, rhythms which the human being feels in the depth of his soul. Don't forget that music is the most elementary among all forms of communication. It is also universal. Perhaps cosmic reality is the manifestation of vibrations, of rhythms, of harmonies and disharmonies. Later when you have read and studied sciences, and particularly the new theory in physics, the "String theory," we can speak about this again.

*   *   *   *   *

Why do people engage in wars? Why do they kill each other?

In our time, we work very hard to prevent wars. We do not always succeed. I hope that when you are my age, armed conflicts will irreversibly belong to the past.

But how can we stop the killings?

One has to start very early. If, for instance, one of your school-mates attacks you, even violently, you have the right to defend yourself, but at the same time you should try to reason with him. Try to understand him, and also to make yourself understood by him.

*   *   *   *   *

I am afraid of terrorism. Practically every day one sees pictures on television of suicide attacks. Are these people desperate?

To a certain extent, yes, they are desperate and frustrated. But it is also the fight of those who want to impose their way of being, their way of thinking which is static. And then there are all those who, in their irrational thinking, believe that terrorism is the only mean to restore injustices. Finally, terrorism is also due to unscrupulous men who use suicidal attacks to their own advantage, driving primitive and desperate young people to these ultimate criminal acts. These terrorist leaders are a minority who themselves live in comfort and luxury by sending others to death and causing the death of innocents.

But there is so much injustice; there are so many social and economic imbalances abounding in our time. What would you propose?

This calls for an in-depth study. I cannot give you a conclusive brief answer, but I am confident that new thinking, new mentalities in particular in the new younger generation, will succeed in correcting and eliminating these imbalances. More and more encounters among young people from different strata of society with an open mind should progressively bring a solution.

*   *   *   *   *

The other day I saw Aunt Lisa. She was crying and she felt desperate. She wanted to speak to the medical doctor who did not have time. Why do doctors not speak to their patients longer? Are they so busy?

Don't forget that the medical doctors take care of their patients to the best of their abilities, but they are very often overwhelmed with work, worn out. Yet they carry on because the vast majority of them have a great sense of responsibility for life and death, which rest on their shoulders. But there are men and women who voluntarily spend part of their time to accompany the sick and listen to them. They do a wonderful job, and they are complementary to the hard and important work of the medical doctors.

*   *   *   *   *

I often ask myself about my future. Shall I find work? This becomes more and more difficult for the younger people. And then what kind of studies should I pursue, and in what professional activities should I engage? Where shall I have the greatest chance of success? Do I need to succeed, by the way?

I have no answer regarding the problem of unemployment. I think we are living in a period of transition, in a period where technology opens new possibilities for the younger generation. Society is practically condemned to find a solution, which appears to be particularly urgent in countries and regions engaged in the process of adaptation to a global world.

This being said, I have no magic solution for professional success. But in my view, what counts is the pleasure which you feel when you wake up in the morning, and you are looking forward to a day at school or a day at work. If a feeling of joy, even bliss, penetrates you when you wake up, then I think you are engaged on a good road. Whether you choose a profession in technology, in agriculture, in banking, in law, in business, in teaching, or even as a simple factory worker, you will feel happiness if your work is in line with your abilities and tastes. Then I think you will have made a good choice. And above all, never forget, my son, that in order to be really happy, you have to share.

The virus "Rumin"

The virus existed for a long, long time. In fact, it has been around since the dawn of humanity. It affects human beings, but strangely enough, not animals. It causes a lot of suffering to those who are the victims, but it brings delight to those who act as transmittal agents from mouth to ear, as well as through communication by mail or by media. The virus does not attack physical organs of human beings but their reputation. It starts to create doubt in the minds, and then it succeeds in causing trouble and finishes by destroying the private, the professional, and the social life of the victim. In extreme cases, the virus might even eliminate lives, driving people to suicide.

This virus is known under the term of "Rumin" which is a contraction of Rumor and Insinuation.

*   *   *   *   *

Five P.M. Reception in one of the high class hotels in town. Mr. V. (like Victim) is among the invitees.

"Hello Mr. V. How are you? You look fine. And what a super, super suntan! This is really not astonishing with the blessed weather we have. One doesn't need to go on vacation abroad. There are so many picturesque unvisited places even in our small country."

"Indeed, that's why we decided, my wife and I, not to go to another country for our vacation. We just stayed at home."

"But that's great! What a good idea to stay home. We, I must say, spent a magnificent fifteen days on the Seychelles Islands.

After all one lives only once, doesn't one? I tell you, paradise on earth, the Seychelles. The children were delighted, absolutely ravished. You should go there for your next holiday trip . . . But I am sorry, I have to apologize. I just saw a friend to whom I absolutely have to speak. In spite of many calls from my mobile phone I did not succeed in reaching him. He must have been abroad. Hope to see you later."

Mr. V., a habitué of these receptions, is rather astonished that tonight many of his old acquaintances with whom he was accustomed to have a conversation either appear to have not seen him, or if they cannot avoid saying hello, they all find an excuse to run off.

Soon, V. leaves the reception.

But what happened to V.? It is just as simple as that: he is under attack by the virus Rumin.

The company he manages is under an official inquiry. This is certainly not exceptional. Quite frequently in the past there have been similar verifications and inquiries. Yet in our time, they are multiplied, I don't know by which factor. V. is not conscious of having violated any regulations or laws, but he has to prove this. Some media indulge with delight in reporting the slightest information or news they think having got from a reliable source.

The inquiries can last months, even years. Fortunately, in our democracies there is a presumption of innocence for those who are accused, at least, in law. But as quite a lot transpires to the outside world through the media or through rumors and whispers, what remains then of the presumption of innocence?

Of course there are friends, the real ones, which one can count on the fingers of one hand. They manifest a certain solidarity with V. They invite him and his wife to dinner, privately and not too often. After all, one has to protect oneself in order not to be drawn into some kind of affair which risks compromising one's own reputation.

For V., this agony lasts two long years. After the inquiry has been concluded, his innocence is established. This is reported by the media in a brief communiqué without any comment.

V. and his family are of course relieved. But contrary to other viral infections, Rumin leaves a sequel of mental scars. V. is not the same anymore. It is true that at the receptions which he no longer has great inclination to attend, he is surrounded again by the party-goers who do not avoid him anymore, and who do not fail to say to each other: "I always said that it was a misunderstanding, and that V. would be cleared of any of the faults he was accused of."

V., with his moral wound still quite open, feels heartened however by such marks of sympathy and as an optimist he hopes that time will heal the moral wound.

One day, upon entering a restaurant, he hears a voice from the end of the room: "There is no smoke without fire!" V. turns his heels and walks out of the restaurant.

He never will know that in fact what he heard was the statement of a patron who believed that he had detected the start of a fire in the kitchen of the restaurant.

*   *   *   *   *

In the afternoon in a cozy coffee shop of a well-known pastry store, two friends meet and have a conversation. The two women are just gossiping a trifle. They exchange some confidences.

"By the way, do you still meet the XY's?"

"Of course, they are friends. Paul and I we are very fond of them. Why do you ask?"

"You know, it's rather delicate. If I speak to you about this, it's because I am your closest friend. I think you should be careful, be on your guard, particularly with regard to her. At a dinner offered by Minister K., when coffee was served, Mrs. XY told me that she has heard from somebody, who is a very serious person, that you have a lover. Don't worry. I told her right away that as I know you, this is impossible. And yet, if it was the case, it is not extraordinary in our time, is it?"

"This is ridiculous. From whom does she pretend to have this information?"

"Ah, that she did not tell me. I've asked quite a number of times, but she did not want to give me an answer. I must say that she appears to have heard this from many sources."

"Many sources, you say? That means that the rumor has already been spread all over town?"

"All over town I don't know. Anyhow, quite a number of people seem to be aware of this."

"But this is just despicable, horrible!"

"Yes, despicable. But that isn't all. On one side, they think that you have a lover, because you lack something at home. Maybe Paul is not capable anymore of satisfying you. Others pretend to have seen Paul in the company of a beautiful young woman at a rather unusual place. As Paul is a very attractive man and in his youth had the reputation to be a lady killer, some pretend that you are having a liaison just to take revenge.

"This is absurd. First of all I have no lover. Then I can assure you, Paul has no virility problems. As for the rest, I am sure of Paul. Let's forget all that. We are losing our time discussing such silly, inane gossip."

"This is also my point of view. But please do understand me. You are my best friend, I just want to warn you regarding the XY's, about the heinous rumor they are spreading, and of which I do not believe the slightest word, of course. This might hurt you, but I think it is best that you are informed. All the more so, since there is also a saying: 'There is no smoke without fire.' "

In the evening, back home, Paul finds his wife a bit distant and he is quite surprised when she asked him point blank: "Do you want tell me something, by any chance?"

A new mentality and a new behavior

Mr. Israel, your short stories deal with major flaws in our society, such as social injustice, boring instead of stimulating education, capital punishment, insinuations, slanders, hypocrisy, and so on. You underline quite rightly that the enumeration of these flaws in our society is far from being complete. Therefore in a more general manner: How do you think that planetary thinking which you advocate could contribute to eliminate injustices, inconsistencies, imbalances, and thus lead us to a better, a more peaceful world?

Changing mentalities and also behavior is not an easy undertaking. It is a process over an extended period of time. I hope that the rather dismal evolution experienced on our planet allows sufficient time to bring about the essential corrections. In his remarkable book, *High Noon: Twenty Global Problems–Twenty Years to Solve Them,* Jean-François Rischard thinks that humanity has only about twenty years at its disposal to deal with the most crucial global problems.

I fully agree with this. One has to act rapidly and with energy, with both traditional as well as innovative measures. We have no time to lose any more. I am convinced that any effective sustainable solution will pass necessarily through new thinking leading to a new mentality.

I mentioned a new vision of the world already in the context of a new perception of reality as it unfolds to us in the present state of knowledge. But this is not sufficient to reach a level of planetary thinking and to bring about a change of mentalities.

Probably since the appearance of life and in particular of *Homo sapiens sapiens* on our planet, our generation has experienced a most fundamental event: putting two men, Armstrong and Aldrin, on the moon. This event of planetary scope with implications for humanity, difficult to imagine in the past, imperatively calls for new holistic thinking. For the first time, human beings detach themselves from earth on which humanity is firmly rooted. Neil Armstrong, while leaving the Lem and putting his feet on the rocky soil of the moon, exclaimed: "That's one small step for man, one giant leap for mankind." I watched this event in 1969 on television. I couldn't believe my eyes when I saw the hesitant, clumsy steps of Armstrong and Aldrin on the moon, their strange choreography due to the lighter gravitational pull of the moon. Breathless, I was drunk with an emotion I cannot describe. I realized that from then on, something had profoundly and fundamentally changed. Our thinking and the way we view reality will be different from now on.

Simultaneously with me, millions and millions of other people watching this event on television must have reacted in the same manner. In our time, those born after us, the younger generation, take this for granted to a certain extent. And so it must be stressed again and again that a new turn has been taken in the evolutionary process of humanity, and more generally of life on our planet. We also have to communicate this feeling of bliss and awe which we experienced suddenly by viewing and by admiring the beauty of our blue planet, which we saw in its splendor for the first time as photographed from outer space and transmitted to us thanks to advanced technology. We suddenly realized that humanity, as diverse as it is, through the variety of cultures, is one single family, the family of man as defined by the Luxembourg American photographer, Edward Steichen. In this new world, there should not and cannot be a place any more for war, killing, and terrorism. A new feeling of solidarity between all human beings has to arise and to strengthen and measures have to be taken to correct social injustices and human sufferings.

The possibilities offered from that moment on are wide open. In fact they are infinite. In prehistoric times, some species left the sea to live on land. This process as described by Darwin has been a long evolution extending over millions and millions of years. Voyages by rockets to outer space and finally putting human beings on the moon have taken place within an incomparable short span of time. This is due to the progress of knowledge, in a constantly accelerating evolution extending not over millions, but only over hundreds and tens of years. The human brain, active with its neurological network, is shortening dramatically the course of evolution to which it gives impetus and a direction. Thus chance and contingency appear to be reduced while a purpose, in the wake of the progress of knowledge, emerges and the unique direction of the arrow of time acquires a profound significance. We have entered the post-Darwinian era, which calls for New Thinking. In our time and in the future, it is those who blend the progress of knowledge with spirituality who will prevail and not those who are the physically and militarily strongest.

On planet earth, Nature is taking a U-turn engaging itself in a bifurcation leading ultimately, in the vision of the priest and philosopher Teilhard de Chardin, to the point Omega, the final destination when humanity will rejoin its Creator.

And all this, in your opinion will solve humanity's problems?

Certainly not by itself. New thinking will be the bedrock on which we can construct a better world.

If such a new vision of the world leading to new mentalities becomes a reality, what do you propose in order to implement the necessary steps and measures for changing our behavior, our way of dealing with our problems, our way of life and thinking in the years, decades and centuries ahead?

The corollary of new planetary thinking is new planetary ethics. The Catholic theologian and philosopher Hans Küng speaks of the "Weltethos," worldwide ethics. In the past, the ethical code regulated the relations between human beings on the scale of a tribe, a community, a city-state as in ancient Greece, and then a nation. Nowadays, mainly through communications, the way we believe and the way we behave has global planetary implications and consequences. Therefore the code of conduct of ethics has to be global, planetary. How to establish and how to implement such a global code of ethics is a major challenge, probably one of the greatest challenges confronting mankind in our time.

Many initiatives have already been taken in this direction. Let me just recall the Council for a Parliament of the world religions which was held in Chicago in 1993, and which proposed a code for planetary ethics.

More recently a group of elder statesmen meeting within the framework of an interactive council submitted to the Secretary General of the United Nations a text called a "Universal declaration of the obligations and responsibilities of individuals." This document stressed not only the human rights but also the human obligations. All these initiatives are important.

As far as I am concerned, I want to confine myself to one major objective: education. The changes I propose for a new vision of the world, a new mentality, and a new behavior, can only be effective if an appropriate education is given first and foremost to our children and to the adolescents, those who build the future, and I would like to add to the elder people. After all, this is a vital topic for lifelong learning. Education must implant in human beings the seed on which a new mentality will arise and unfold.

Thus in a more general manner, education must place more emphasis on the level of knowledge which we have reached at present, and upon which we shall construct the future, rather than relating the history of the acquisition of knowledge. Then it should be communicated with insistence and an appropriate documentation that humanity is a whole composed of many cultures and many civilizations bound together, more than ever before, by a planetary solidarity. The ways and means have to be identified to eliminate wars and to put a halt to the demographic explosions as well the pollution of our environment.

The sanctuaries of the future will no longer be monuments in stones but the landmarks in the progress of knowledge and peaceful coexistence encompassing the whole of humanity. The American sociologist and visionary, Alvin Toffler, in his remarkable book *Powershift*, shows and explains that the future belongs not to the physically or militarily strongest but to those who will have acquired a maximum of knowledge utilizing it in the interest of the whole community.

It must be underlined that wars are not inevitable. There are no holy wars; only life is holy. The Roman saying "Si vis pacem, para bellum" (*If you want peace, prepare war*) must be universally replaced by the commandment "Si vis pacem, para pacem" (*If you want peace, prepare peace*). For the educator, transmitting knowledge, explaining science and research, must be an activity he performs with joy, with pleasure and even with enthusiasm. These feelings must be transmitted to the students, to those with whom he is engaged in the process of a constructive dialogue and exchange of views.

In this educational process, it must be constantly stressed that, for instance, the findings in science and scientific research have reached a certain level of our understanding and can never be considered as the absolute truth. According to the philosopher of science, Karl Popper, real science can be defined as such if it can be proven wrong. Let me just illustrate the pitfalls to which a misconception of science, considering it an absolute truth, can lead, causing important social disruption. For instance, quite recently some neuroscientists postulated that decisions we think to have taken by our own free will, and for which we have to assume our personal responsibility, are in fact manifestations of our neurosystem, preceding by split seconds our act. Thus, there would be no personal accountability. Such findings, if legitimized by our legal and judiciary systems, could lead to conditions which would completely disrupt the fabric of our society. Therefore the following caveat imposes itself. In science there is no absolute truth and what is considered to be demonstrated today can be disproved and will be disproved tomorrow. In this context, the definition of science by Popper should always be present in our mind.

Yes, humanity is irreversibly embarked on the road of progressive knowledge. We are mountain climbers, moving on slippery soil. We have to avoid the dangers which confront us and yet at each stop, new challenges wait for us and we go on climbing and climbing, trying to reach a summit, the ultimate truth, which seems to recede the more we think that we are in its proximity.

That is the destiny of mankind. It is particularly fascinating, because climbing on this road, we continuously reap the benefits of our efforts through a better life, through better health conditions, through the lengthening of the average life span.

In conclusion, such an attitude, born out of a new mentality and a new sense of global responsibility, leaves wide open the field of a fruitful exchange of views and ideas between those who belong to organized religions, those who are philosophers, and also those who are scientists and who say that for them the cosmos is a vast, not understandable chaos without any guiding principles, without any significance.

In Western civilization knowledge has progressed and evolved through science rooted in the Hellenistic philosophy to approach reality.

Other cultures have developed their own vision of reality in the wake of their traditions and beliefs, leading to a variety of creeds and philosophies. Though the effectiveness of the scientific approach appears to be amply proven, it would be wrong and counterproductive to impose it on other cultures as the only way to grasp reality.

I am convinced that the essence of New Thinking is the irreversibility of time pointing in one direction, forward: forward in the wake of the universal dynamic process of evolution. "Nothing is permanent but change" and values, though eternal, have to be redefined and reinterpreted in a constantly, and in our time of transition, fast-changing environment.

The relations between individuals and nations have to be based on the principle that reality is not static and what was considered as absolute truth yesterday is not necessarily true today. This appears to me the only way to fight efficiently and without bloodshed terrorism generated by fundamentalist static thinking. The concept of the unidirectional arrow of time should be part of the educational programs.

A study could be conducted on the practical application on a day-to-day basis of these principles as well as on ethics, the permanent guide for the behavior of man with his neighbor. Thus the message of the prophets and of Jesus–"Love thy neighbor as you love yourself"–will find its accomplishment.

Descartes says: "I think, therefore I am." The believer says: "I believe, therefore I am." I am tempted to say: "I love, therefore I am."

And it is to love, to my love for life that I dedicate the following last short story.

At a colloquium which took place in Luxembourg in the year 2000 on "Higher education in a knowledge-based society," a professor of a well known university in Hong Kong said in a jesting manner: "We, the scientists, are sometimes a little wacky. Thus we could even imagine and postulate that in a distant future, thinking will exist and evolve without any organic support."

This statement has inspired me to write the following story.

In Love with Life

On a Saturday afternoon there was scorching heat in Luxembourg. Schmitt decided to take a drink on a terrace of the Place d'Armes. There were many people there, and a rock band played passionate rhythms. At Schmitt's table there was a free seat. A man approached, clad in an elegant suit completely out of place in the torrid heat. He sat down without uttering a single word. Schmitt observed him silently. He was tall, slim with ample dark brown hair, his face very harmonious, recalling the works of art of the ancient Hellenistic sculptors. The waiter asked him what he would like to drink. The man looked quizzically around him and then with his elegant index finger he pointed to the bottle of mineral water of Schmitt. Once served, he did not touch it in spite of the heat. He turned his head incessantly in all directions and appeared to carefully register everything which happens around him. All of this with a detached look. His eyes were like an icy lake reflecting a blue sky on a sunny day.

Suddenly he addressed himself politely to Schmitt:

"May I ask you: What is this country and what is this town?"

Surprised by this unexpected question, Schmitt asked him, slightly ruffled:

"But sir, you came here. You must know that you are in Luxembourg, and here is the capital of Luxembourg, which is also called Luxembourg."

"Thank you very much. I just wanted verification. Thanks for the information."

The stranger continued with his roving eyes to observe the crowd strolling leisurely. Schmitt noticed that contrary to everyone, the stranger did not perspire. Moved by an increasing curiosity, he decided to ask a question which was literally burning his lips:

"Excuse me, sir. May I ask you from where you come?"

"Oh, that would be too long and complicated to explain."

"I understand. I don't want to be indiscreet. In Luxembourg, we are very discreet; you know the banking secret and so on."

"What does that mean, banking secret?"

"Banking secret is a specific form of confidentiality regarding financial matters."

"I see. Thank you very much for the information. Very interesting."

"You must like this expression."

"Every new word pleases me. It is information, and every piece of new information is important for me."

"Oh yes. What do you do with all this information, may I ask you?"

"I record it. I analyze it. I compare it, and if it is good information I try to draw out of it new information by extrapolation, deduction, induction . . ."

"I understand. But why do you do that? Is that your profession?"

The other was silent for a few seconds, and then he cast his translucent look at Schmitt.

"As you appear to be really interested, I shall tell you, but you probably won't believe me. That is why, a few moments ago, I did not want to reply to your question regarding my origin. But before reacting, listen to me carefully. Of course I count on your discretion. I come from a distant galaxy. In the course of my peregrinations through space and time, I find myself here to collect information on your planet and its inhabitants."

Schmitt is flabbergasted. He thinks that he is in front of a mentally deranged man. Yet curiosity drives him on to pursue the conversation.

"Well, you come from a distant galaxy. However, in our universe, distances between galaxies can be measured in millions of light years. According to Einstein, it is impossible to exceed the speed of light, which is about 300,000 kilometers per second. I would be interested to hear how you came to Luxembourg and by all appearances in good shape?"

"The law of gravitation does not apply to us. We are dematerialized beings. At the state of evolution we have reached, there only remains the immaterial part, the thought. We have no body. This allows us to move practically instantaneously in space and time whatever the distances. In principle, you have the same capacity as we. But your thought is still imprisoned in your body, as was the case on our planet, a long, long time ago."

"But you, in front of me, you have a body. You wear clothes."

"That's an illusion which is projected around us for the comfort of our intergalactic interlocutors. As a matter of fact, we are pure thoughts, thus eternal. We shed our organic shell. If you touch me, if we shake hands, you will notice that."

Schmitt, shaking hands with the stranger, did not feel anything. Yet he presented himself:

"My name is Schmitt, and what's yours?"

"I have no name. If you wish you can call me Alpha, or rather Omega."

Schmitt was very upset. He did not know what to say and excused himself while he went to the toilet. Only after a relatively long time he returned and spoke to Omega in a whispering voice:

"Well, it's true then? You are an authentic extraterrestrial being. Right from the start, I noticed something special about you. And for you there are no distances. It's unbelievable. And you are immortal if I understand you correctly?"

"Of course."

"Fantastic. And what do you do in this timeless, eternal existence?"

"We collect, analyze, and process information. This is natural for conscientious thoughts."

"But this must be very boring to collect and treat information from here to eternity?"

"Our task is to collect information and to process it, that's all."

"You do that for which purposes?"

"To enrich our intellectual heritage, our vast database of information."

"And what in the last resort do you do with your database of stocked up knowledge?"

"We enrich it continuously, as I explained to you. And that's the reason of my presence here."

"And that's all?"

"Why do you want more? Listen Schmitt, be a bit rational. We are pure thoughts. What do you wish us to do with our intellectual heritage? We have no body . . ."

"Precisely! I try to be rational. I am asking myself if it would not be an advantage for you to have a body and to be mortal rather than accumulating and processing information. Then you could contribute to the construction of a real world, unfinished and permanently in the making."

"By roaming over your planet, and having noticed so many explosions, so many war machines, so many killings, I must say that I feel rather relieved not to have your faculty to construct what you call the real world."

"It is true that wars and other ills still proliferate on our planet, but they are also a challenge. Humanity slowly and in many zigzag movements works constantly to construct a better world. This is our destiny, a difficult one but also an inspiring one. We are builders in time: you do not build, and you miss a most exhilarating feeling, the fascinating task to build for which we need our bodies."

"OK. But in contrast, you are mortal."

"That is a rather unilateral view of things. You do not consider Love in all your reasoning."

"We are rational beings, Schmitt. For us, Love is out of question; or rather it does not exist. This does not prevent us from recording and analyzing all information, including Love."

"I do not want to know what your analysis means to you. You have no bodies, no sensations, no emotions, you cannot know what Love is; it is beyond your understanding. Thanks to the fusion of individuals who love themselves and procreate in Love, life renews itself continuously. Death is powerless. It puts an end to individual lives, but it is unable to block the permanent linking in the process of life. Love is stronger than death."

"This is an interesting reasoning. To my knowledge, our analysis never reached that point. I shall deal with this personally in order to update our database."

"While analyzing and updating perhaps you could ponder on the following features: death puts an end to our individual life but at the same time it renders life more intense. Happiness is a fleeting moment. We feel it when the sun at dawn is rising on the horizon, when a child is being born, in the kiss of a beloved one, in the creation of works of art. We are untiring searchers of happiness. Bad luck, sadness, and grief do not change us fundamentally, because searching for happiness is already a source of happiness. You really don't know what you miss in your existence of thoughts."

"Such a question does not pose itself to us. We are rational beings. We shall of course integrate all this information in our heritage. Is there anything else I should know for instance on Love which appears to me a particularly interesting information?"

"But you never understand anything of Love, as you have no body, no sensations, and no feelings. You cannot feel pleasure. You do not laugh. And Love under its various, I would even say infinite, forms is so vast . . . Look, there are a couple of lovers sitting two tables away from us. They look at each other with tenderness. They fondle each other, they kiss each other. It's moving, isn't it?"

"It's very interesting, but yet, their Love is evanescent because they will die."

"When aging, they of course painfully feel death approaching. But they will love each other even more intensely, aware that the beautiful adventure comes to an end. In the meantime they don't think of death. They want to be happy. Do you know what it means to be happy, Omega?"

154 / NEW THINKING

Omega, obviously forgetting to pay for his mineral water, gets up and leaves in silence. Slowly he passes the table of the two lovers and for the first time there appears in his eyes a kind of nostalgic feeling.

Schmitt pays for the two mineral waters. Returning home, he is thoughtful. Yes, he is also a being who thinks like Omega, but he is also a being who has a body, who loves, who is happy, yet knowing that he will die one day.

And more intensely than ever, Schmitt loves life, is passionately **In Love with Life**.

Biographical Note

Edmond Israel was born in Luxembourg and is of Luxembourg nationality. After a long and distinguished career in international banking with Banque Internationale à Luxembourg, now called Dexia BIL, and as Founding Chairman of Cedel International, now called Clearstream International, he became Chairman of the Luxembourg Stock Exchange in 1989 and held the post of President of the Federation of European Stock Exchanges from 1993 to 1995. In 1998, he was elected Vice-Chairman and in 1999 Chairman of the Board of Governors of the Asia-Europe Foundation. He has received numerous international honors from universities, governments, and other public bodies in recognition of his contribution to culture, the financial markets, and Luxembourg.